The Re

(life beyond)

Edwin Rivera

PublishAmerica
Baltimore

First printing

PublishAmerica has allowed this work to remain exactly as the author intended, verbatim, without editorial input.

Hardcover 978-1-4560-6456-3
Softcover 978-1-4560-6455-6
PUBLISHED BY PUBLISHAMERICA, LLLP
www.publishamerica.com
Baltimore

Printed in the United States of America

Dedicated to my sister, I love you very much.

Mayda I. Rivera
July 1, 1953-January 18, 2008

"to our mother, we love and miss you so much, your children"
Carmen your daughter

"mother of courage, miss you dearly, on my mind everyday, hoping to see you sooner than later"
Melinda your daughter

"I miss your unconditional love and acceptance"
Beverly your daughter

"all that I am in life, I owe to my Angel mother"
Santos your son

"mom I love and miss you, love always your son"
Little Luis

Table of Contents

There is a place that I have always known to exist. As I walk through its gates I am at awe at its beauty. The walls are constructed with marble and diamonds of colors that I have never seen before. The light that shines through its walls is not like the light of the sun but it is like the light that the bible mentions. I hear the sounds of music as I look straight ahead to its corridors of majestic beauty. As I continue to walk, I finally reach a door made of some sort of heavenly steel. I open the door that is as durable as steel but as light as a feather. In the room, there is yet another corridor with the same design as the entrance that I walked through. In that corridor there are hundreds of walls. One particular wall that I see has the name, Wall of Remembrance.

On the wall, I see the names of great writers that came from earth. I am astonished at its beauty and at its presentation of its writers. Suddenly, at the bottom of the wall I see my name. As I get a teary eye and I gasp for air I hear my name being called. I look towards the corridor where the light is coming from. I see a man walking towards me and calling me by my name. He appears to be dressed in white and bare footed. Then as he asks for my hand and leads me, I see myself being transformed. I am now dressed in white clothing and barefooted like him. He leads the way through the biggest doors that I have ever seen. As I walk through the entrance, I see a name written on the doors of this entrance. It reads "the light of the world". There, an angel with wings curled up in an upright position approaches me. He hands me a writing tool. The tool is made of some sort of marble stone and some kind of granite substance. The colors on this instrument are that of rainbow colors. This writing instrument is light as a feather when I hold it in my hands. Then a voice says to me that I am a writer and that I will join a company of writers to write at this place called The Realm of Writers.

There are many reasons why people do the things they do in life. I write in these times because I escape the daily battles and it allows me to remember and know that God is with me. I realize that life tortures us in many different ways. The writings are for some to be real, and others not to be real. As you read the writings in this book you will read things that you may question my belief. Understand that I wrote this so that you may see that although I believe in whom I believe in, I too am human and I too come short of His glory. In my life, as a writer I go to that dimension where very few writers go. There are no educational institutions there. There are no scholars there. There are no programs there. There is just the creation of your mind. This dimension is not of earth but it is out of earth. It is a place, where many writers dream of going, wish of going, but few dare to go. I am here now and I send this message to others out there. I am here, at a place called The Realm of Writers.

To the World and Back

Realm of Writers

It is a sanctuary of past, present and future writers.
It is a sanctuary of writers from earth.
To this fortress, they come as time travelers.
They come as lovers of literature.
They come as walkers of the earth.
They come as admirers of beauty.
In this Realm of Writers, they come to seek refuge.
In this place writers write their fears.
Writers write their fantasies.
Writers write their hate.
To this realm, I come as *A Writer of Time*.
Seeking the comfort and liberty to write
the love that is inside of me. For even I, full of joy and talent
have met God in this
place of literature. For God has shown himself to be a writer
in this place.
I like this place of peace, this place of beauty, this place of
challenge.

Her Story

She was a person that came on a day full of grace.
I remember her by her silky black hair and her deep smile.
I had a sister that came to this earth as if with butterfly
wings.
She stood beautiful more often than not, beautiful over, and
over like the woman she was. She came from a place called
heaven, and came with heavenly company to this earth. As
she grew older throughout the years, she built a legacy that
will forever endure. Today I stand here saying that from the
sky above she branded herself forever in our hearts. As the
age on earth passes on, we should know that a sister of mine
came to earth and influenced us all. Over, and over I see her
smile, I see her eyes, and I even remember her wonderful
voice. She touched many but many did not see her wonderful
story that dwelled within her. She came to earth for a short
while, and was with us just long enough to remind us of
how good He is. My sister Mayda held us in her arms, not
just like a mother but also much like who she was. She
lived on earth long enough to leave her legacy so that we
would all remember why her story was. I tell you my family,
my friends, and my God. Mayda gave us so much that we
could not understand. However, on that day when she stood
on mount Victory, she was dressed all in white with her
silky black hair. As God took his daughter and raised her in
his arms, she said to us all how much love means to God.
Her story was long and short on this earth and it certainly
touched us all. My sister spoke to me not as a man, but she
spoke to me as her brother with love. My sister told me her
story as I watched her life unfold before my eyes. Even in
her last days on earth, she told her story with passion as God

was with her; and on that day during that moment of glare, with her family and children by her side, we saw the story that she was trying to tell us of her life. That life is about love, and loving each other forever more. Let the mistakes go on and on, while love conquers our hearts so much more. I stand here to write these strong words about her story that my sister Mayda left to us all. Pursue happiness with those whom you have. Pursue the love that comes from above. Do not ever forget that her story was strong. Mayda my dear, we will see you soon because you are not far. Until then my beautiful sister, stand in his presence telling your story that was so precious to us all. We think of you as a pillar in our hearts. Thank you for the love that you gave to us all. When I look towards heaven and I see the blue sky, I can only remember the beauty of your life. The legacy you left you did not just leave behind, but gave to this world to know that your children carry you inside. Thank you, sister for all the years that you gave to us all. Thank you for your story that was so true, so true to us all.

The Color of Love

You gave the kiss of life.
You gave the look of love.
When, I saw you walking down that strip of life.
You gave me that sense of love.
As you walked you danced your way into my heart.
As you gave me the look of a friend, I was touched forever.
You gave me that kiss of life.
You gave me that kiss of love.
On that evening when you approached me by the wall of love.
You made me blush, you made me stop, and you made me kiss you for life.
Right then and there you gave me the color of love.

Amazement

I am amazed at what you have done in my life.
All that I am and all that I have is because of you.
Every morning when I get up I am amazed at the
family you have given to me. I am amazed at the promotions
you have provided to me. In the middle of the day
when I stop to catch my breath I am amazed at your mercy. I
am
amazed at your grace and the abundance of your
love when I fail you. I am amazed at how you travel me to
places that I cannot go on my own. You are amazing. You are
my God
and I worship you. I want you to know that I love
you. I belong to you. I am amazed.

A Crystal Moment of Love

The road to life is clear for some and dark for others.
You came to my road as a visitor.
I, being the dark creature that I was, I hesitated to
understand. I came across you my lord on that day,
on that dark road I came to know you. I noticed that on that
road as you gave me life and as you started to walk that your
steps made the road crystallized. The light that comes from
your very being is life itself. You are magnificent my lord. I
stand here alive because of you. You are the good lord. You
are the savior. I don't have life figured out, but you oh lord,
you fill my heart with great joy and assurance. The moments
I have of death you give to me of life. The enemies that he
sends to kill me you send them to bless me. You even offer
salvation to those that wrong me. Yet I see mercy in my heart
because of what I have seen in yours. Lord, I love you my
father. May you always and forever reign in my life! May
all that I have, all that I am and all that I come across on this
earth of old! Be yours to keep. Truly you are my God. On
that road I was crystallized.

Face book conversation with Chris

2:49am "Life is hard Tio"
2:51am "there are certain laws of life that will always work"
2:51am "like?"
2:54am "no matter what anyone has said says or will say
it is a chain reaction that the world has, but made by god that
will accommodate our life"
2:55am "so wut is it"
2:56am "and the only way you and me and others can see it
and join it is by sitting back and letting it happen
like when the bible says ask that mountain to move and it
will if u have faith
what that means is not just faith in god, but in you and in
the nature of the mountain to move cause Jesus said, greater
works you will do in my name because I must go back to the
father so life has a healing mechanism for when we come
across the life is hard part of our life for example when the
recession came I was taught to go out on the limb and spend
more but have less to gain a lot go through fire so that you
can walk on water take in life so that you can give life back
eat what you need but don't eat to please your flesh
play for the love of the moment but not for the glory of
others
do favors and assist for their sake and not yours
help others and you will be helped always
let loose so that you can heal old wounds and so that new
ones will come
if you must fight, fight to win but not to destroy cause then
you will have no company of good things to come
meaning we will always have and need enemies in the world
aim for perfection but know that in that attempt you are

showing how imperfect u are
realize that time is ticking and your job and time here on
earth will be done, but not in vain pass on the baton
nothing belongs to you but it belongs to God and the life here
that u have also
so sometimes when u do something out of the ordinary
way of life what will happen is you will hear life and it will
respond to you."
3:09am "that's deep!"
3:10am "yea maybe…best I can do to explain it."
3:11am "luv you kid…"

Tranquility

Tranquil the night stands as such. Nothing like the whispers of the
tranquil sea. The tranquil breeze soothes our woes. The movement of
the untamed air seeks its refuge. Then out of the shores of it's heavenly
sandy beach. It shows itself to be true. The Caribbean sun welcomes us
home. The tranquility of the island overwhelms us.

A Once In a Life Time Moment

Across from the Earth's corridor, I saw her. She was smooth walking onto
Stardom. I saw her that day in Century of beauty. She stared at me as I
introduced myself. I looked at her Onyx colored eyes. She looked at me with a
lady's smile and I told her a story. She never saw it coming. She never saw it
before. She thought that it was a fluke as this body guard had never pursued the
moment. I stood there at my post with my Sun glasses to hold back the glare of
stardom that came from her. I stood there looking at her eyes as she could not
believe what I was telling her. On that night, she knew that someone on earth
spoke to her from the heart. No voice, no literature. Just a heart beat and the
stare from where I was standing. Then suddenly as it was almost all over, as she
once again stood a few feet away, I leaned towards her, grabbed her hand, and
whispered into her ear. Then right at that moment, her Onyx colored eyes told
the story. She was that person on that moment. A once in a life time moment!
AKA *The body Guard*

True Love

My comfort in life is to love.
Love is the very essence of God.
From the beginning to the end, love bounds on us humans.
Some take it serious. Some do it in lust. Many abuse this love.
Liars came in many forms. Reality tells me. Be aware of this woman's love.
However, God tells me-abide in him for his word is truth. So today, I tell you.
I love you-friend, sister, you, my girlfriend.

Before You Think of Throwing Me Away, Read Me!

Let me tell you of the living God!
Romans 6: 23 says: "For the wages of sin is death, but the gift of God is eternal life through Jesus Christ our Lord." God wants to have a relationship with you! You can start by giving your life to Jesus Christ: Pray this prayer, Father I pray confessing my sins to Jesus Christ and believe that Jesus is your Son and that he died on the cross for my sins. I believe that he was raised from the dead by you God. Father, help me get closer to you. Jesus I give my life to you. "Amen." God bless you.

The Cave of Souls

I stood on that day to see the tragedy that had occurred.
From the far eastern shore came a man dressed in white.
Overtaken by life's most unique challenges he requested a
gift.
The gift was to be given by the villagers whom resided there.
As the villagers denied this gift, the man in rage cursed and
vanished the village.
When the years ran out at that village, another man came to
claim a gift.
As he was to request this gift, he found out that no human
was there to provide that gift. Then he looked to the north
and he saw the first man in disgrace and tormented. The man
was on the north plains with his wings cut off. He was the
one that was kicked out of heaven because of what he had
done. As the other man looked to the north, he saw the first
man's evil ways and demented mind. He is the fallen one. He
is the once angel of disgrace. He was the once jewel of the
morning sky. Now, he is the enemy of our soul that dwells in
the cave.

Family

I cannot tell you how much I love my family.
I sit at night at my table writing about them all.
They are like a melody in the night when there is no room
for sleep.
When the pain in my heart grows because of the wounds
that I have suffered, my family I think of them to ease my
pain. Over and over tears swell in my eyes as I succumb to
the beauty of my family. I also think under this pain about
my wonderful father. I remember the days that he showed
me how wonderful having this family is. He taught us that
by being many that our love would grow strong. I think
that my brothers and sisters have a little bit of my father.
I feel that every single one of my family members gives a
little of themselves to all of us. I grow old now these days
looking upon all of them. I have seen the hurting in all of us
throughout the years. Life has taken a toll on us. And so I see
the end as well as the beginning. I do not have children to
say that on my last day they will be there to say goodbye to
me. Yet, God has assured me that my family will not forget
about me on that day. Neither will God forget about me.
Family is all about the issues, the pain, and the love in this
journey called life. Family is love and my family I love them
deeply.

Tender Years

I stand still in the middle of the tender years
I remember when as a child the tender years were clear
I stand still at awe at the tender years
I feel the days of prosperity in my spirit with the tender years
As I walk to the altar I cannot help but to see those tender
years
You have been magnificent in the tender years
I ask that you would allow my family of younger tender
years to remember me
As I pass on from these tender years to the next allow me to
be in my family's memory
Oh I am at awe at these tender years that I have had
Your presence day in and day out has allowed us to dance the
day and night away as tender years
I have known you now for a short time in these tender years
Yet I feel the movement in my heart that I have been
pardoned of all my mistakes
This all occurred in the tender years of my life
I thank you for those and these tender years
My beloved friend the most highest and everlasting of love
The tender years came out of your goodness and friendship
I am still at awe on this day on this tender year
I do not have to wish that you were here so that you would
ease that pain and so that you would wash away the tears that
I have shed but because you are so great and have already
cleansed me
I see the tender years clearly before my eyes
I am still at awe from these tender years
Oh yes I am still
I exit this world knowing that the tender years came from
you

Time Is Not Forever, Forever Is Time

As I walk through this moment of life.
The way of life swings into my path.
It reminds me, for the times that I come across it.
That time is not forever, yet once it passes by me, time ticks
with the fury of pain.
Again, as it comes near, it reminds me that time is not
forever and never is forever.
At the end, when I am tired of living, worn out, in a state of
mind that I do not want.
It gives me the final answer that, although time is not forever,
forever is time.

A Guy Name Shorty

Shorty came across from another place.
He was a gangster from the other side of the tracks.
We came across each other one night when the road was
dark.
Shorty was who he was.
I came across Shorty on that year when I made a decision.
Then one day when I went to school, I was given the news
that Shorty had left.
As I heard the news, it made me feel sad.
Shorty came across my path that was not right.
Shorty was a guy that I new and I saw come and go.

A Path Written

She was a writer that was to be.
On her path towards the stars, she came to know.
It was that woman that came across the writing works of old.
Her name was unique and her writings rare.
To understand her path, one needed to know life with a dare.
From the island she came to bless our way.
As her poems touched many, many did not even say.
Julia De Burgos was a poet and a writer from that place.
She died on a sidewalk because of the love that never came.
I so much would off enjoyed to have known her, to let her
know that someone on earth appreciates her works.
For this woman was here on earth for only thirty-nine years
to stay.
Her writings are unique like a sparrow designed to win.
I sit at night under the cool moment of a writer's thought.
Thinking of how she could have been if she would have
lived longer on this earth of old.
A unique writer she was, a unique author she became, a
unique person that I never knew. Perhaps, love took her
there, perhaps, shame took her life, or perhaps it was her
writing that carried her to heaven. Today I thank her for all
the writing works that she left here on this earth. You were
special Julia De Burgos. You were unique in the little time
that you lived here on earth.

What to Wish For

As I stand in the midst of my family.
God prompts me as to how to think about the moment.
I look around and I see my nephews, nieces, brothers, and
sisters. I also see friends all around me. I stare at them and
tears form in my eyes. I talk to God about that moment and
he talks back to me. I hear in the room conversations of all
types. Again, I stare at my family. The hours move on and
on as the get together comes to an end. Then suddenly as I
am driving home, God asks me, what I want. I stare at him
sitting next to me and with tears in my eyes. I let God know
that I have nothing to wish for. All that a man could want
in the world I have. A family, full of loved ones and God's
goodness everywhere. No money, no status quo, and no other
thing can match what I have. Then God asks me to stop the
car and let him out at another family's home. Thank, you
God for everything.

A Valiant Man

A unique way of life I see in him.
The day to day living he proves to be strong.
With his black and light gray hair, I see the wisdom that God
has given him.
His simple walk with a sudden twitch of his shoulder, I
remember him.
In his eighty's he stands tall and firm.
A magnificent philosophy of life he has.
Even as he builds his homes, his courage is obvious.
I travel to the island in the Caribbean Sea to see him.
Even his poetry is strong and full of light.
Not only has he been a great man.
Victor Rivera Vazquez has been a great uncle.
I have met great men in my life.
This man has influenced my life.
Truly, he is a valiant man.

A Puerto Rican Sparrow

From a distant place called Boquerón, she is from.
With the flavor of a Puerto Rican icon, she is known.
Her speech is romantic in her own way.
Her talk is impactful.
Her look is of poetic beauty.
Her culture is unique as a sapphire in her ways.
The sparrow that comes from this place where she lives is
herself.
She is like a Greek Goddess.
As if from a fantastic, fantasy story.
Even the glean in her eyes is from a poet that comes from a
place called The Realm of Writers. I encountered this poet in
a place called Boquerón.
In the twilight of the day, she invaded my mind with poetic
rhythmic lessons. She is what we call in this place, a Master
Poet. She is a teacher of poetry; a writing instrument that is
used by a higher being. On that day when I came across a
portal of history, I understood why this woman is a Sparrow.
She even gleams a touch of the great Julia De Burgos. I
came across this sparrow on that day. She is a woman that
the world knows as Myrna Lluch. She is a poet and a Puerto
Rican Sparrow.

The Way of the Warrior

A stand of power.
A cunning strike.
The morning rises and he fights.
The dusk arrives and he rests.
The sword he carries is of devastation.
He is fast.
He is furious.
He is Metsedek.
The way of the warrior!

Music from the Man

In the still of the night, I listen.
In my heart, I hear his lyrics.
It is in my blood my country's blessing of songs.
Oh, how much I love to listen to the songs of Hector Lavoe.
As I am driving my car, I put on the music that moves me.
My country has the most beautiful songs. My country has the
most attractive lyrics. My mind is in a trance when I listen
to that music. I become one with the music when I listen to
it. My country has given birth to great singers of Salsa. He
was a unique singer of our time. When I listen to his music,
I hear Puerto Rico speak. My country gave birth to a singer
of our time. He was from Ponce, a cantante that was unique.
Hector, Hector, you move my heart to know who I am. The
music from this man speaks to the heart. The music from the
man, that every one called Hector Lavoe lives forever.

Unknown Poet

The epitaph was written by the Kings of old.
It seemed as a wrath that once came to the earth made of
gold.
A creature of a man told tales of this poet of old.
He wrote poetry in a time when man saw revenge as it was
told.
The writer created written works for mankind to seek
the truth from a book of old. He wrote it on the walls of
remembrance in a city called Molgatha.
It is told that this poet was seen walking to and from, writing
his belief on the walls of old. He for told, the spiritual way
out of the damnation of the man of old. As he sculpted his
writings on the stones of gold, mankind was astonished at his
accuracy that he for told. Then one hundred of a year old, as
the sky darkened and lightning came to the earth of old. He
vanished as if taken to rest upon a throne of the Kings of old.
Till this day his epitaph was written to tell of his works that
came from a place unknown. It read Unknown Poet.

Yesterday Was a Moment of Truth

The strongest of men faced at a tabernacle of strength
As it was disputed the actions of the warriors of strength
At the city of truth they came together to decide the path for
the time of war
So it came to the day on yesterday's moment that they came
to know the truth
As the men prepared for war on that moment where it was to
come
The decision was final and so the men departed to the ranks
for war
As one of the men walked into the station for his weapon
He looked to his right where a sword made of steel and
marble laid on the floor
At the end of the sword there were three diamonds with three
pearls
As he remembered yesterday's decision of truth
He began to understand that the sword had its power from
the circle of truth on that day
It was love and duty that brought the men together to go to
war against an enemy of old
Yesterday was the moment that the men came together and
learned of the truth

The Battle of the Titans

Cambridge rode his horse across the plains of Galbothia.
As he rode his horse through the country side, he could not
help but to see the destruction by the evilest. The devastation
was noticeable for hundreds of miles.
As he reached his destination, by the river of *Solometh*,
he was met by the titans of Galbothia. Every one of them
lined up to meet with their King of arms. Every one of them
armed with their best since the beginning of their time.
The King rode his horse in the middle of the lines of salute
by his champions. They stood there some on their horses
and some standing on their mighty size. King Cambridge
raised his sword towards the sky. As the sword was aiming
towards the sky, over the hills of Galbothia came the enemies
of Galbothia. They rode their evil horses dressed in black
clothing with their weapons drawn. So it was the Titans
versus the Titans; a battle that was never to be forgotten. The
battle of the titans!

Missing You

I sit thinking of you.
Day in and day out, my heart cries for you.
At night I cannot sleep as I miss you.
I remember the conversations I had with you.
I thought that we would never be apart.
There is a part in my heart that is empty.
Ever since you left to go to heaven, I miss you greatly.
I am sad, very sad over your absence.
I cry over and over thinking of you.
I am your son. I will forever be your son.
I miss you so much. I love you very much.
Your absence is felt greatly in my heart.
You were the best father a son could ever ask for.
I miss you greatly.

Tree

I walked to this tree amongst other trees.
The tree was in front of a fountain illuminated by fire winds.
It was a sight that I had never seen before.
As I approached the tree, I was elevated in the air.
I held to a branch and forced myself down to the ground.
At the trunk of the tree I saw an opening with milk pouring
out of it.
So I took the milk in my hands.
It smelled as sweetness and honey together.
The aroma was pleasing to my senses.
So I decided to drink some of this milk.
As I drank this milk I looked to my right and my left.
I saw other trees, with the same color as this tree.
Then I looked behind me and there he was staring at me,
a serpent standing with its wondering and evil eyes.
It folded its arms and whispered to me.
I could not hear the serpent as the winds of the air made
noise.
So I drank more of this milk from the tree.
Suddenly, as I stared at this serpent my body commenced to
shake.
I was in pain. I was in a moment of hurt.
Again the serpent stared at me with his eyes.
Then from amongst the other trees I heard a great noise.
I saw the branches of the trees move. I felt the ground where
I stood next to the trees, shake. Then he showed himself to
me. As he spoke with his mighty voice, I saw the serpent
under his right foot. Then when he stared at me with his
beautiful eyes, I saw the serpent no more. The trees had
vanished. The wind was settled. The milk and honey did not
exist anymore. So I left this place of once beauty. I gathered
us together and went on the road of repentance. Ever since
that day the trees have stop being trees. Ever since that day, I
have not been the same.

Live and Let Die

The guitar assembles the lyrics.
The voices work overtime to sing.
He sings about that woman.
She drives him crazy as the day starts and ends.
He sees in his mind her curved body.
He draws her glazed lips.
His guitar raises its tone as he imagines her walking.
Even her beauty sings music to him.
Over and over he tells her to live and let die.
It goes higher and higher.
The noise is out of control.
Suddenly, the music stops.
He is all alone.

No Air

How am I supposed to breathe?
She consumes all of my breath.
At night she loves me to almost the end.
When I curve my lips I see them all over her body.
Tell me how am I supposed to breathe?
Our love exhausts our life.
The way she dresses. The way she is, she is a woman.
I walk the beaches of Puerto Rico with her. I see the beauty
that is hers.
Ok, it is the morning and again we go at it. It is love to the
end.
Our love has no air.

The Burning Sphere

Crew members from a night
A dream not a nightmare
A dance as it was called
A style perhaps
We danced the night away
The burning sphere cools the dancing soul
Burns the spirit of one's dancing urge

Lil Suzy

She sang take me in your arms.
It was a trance song.
It hypnotized you.
It would take you in her arms.
It would not let you go.
That piece was great.
A lover's song.
A way to sing forever in her arms.
She did it again.

The Rainforest

It rains raindrops of music.
Listen to the melody of love.
It sparks about love to you.
Can you feel that rhythm of soul?
The cool of the night after a hot summer day!
The rainforest takes you in. It soothes your soul.

Life

Life is unique in all of us.
I find that life has many secrets.
Life to me is to laugh, enjoy and love.
Earth is a garden with God's creations full of life.
The rivers, oceans, mountains, lakes, creatures and so much
more full of life.
A friend once told me "Edwin, always make friends where
ever you go"
I live the dream every day.
A dream full of great people and their accomplishments!
I thank God for what he has done in my life. Life truly is
wonderful. My
family and friends are unique to me. Even in the most
challenging of days, my
life is a wonderful life. I thank the good Lord for making me
a person that is to
be with my friends and family. Life truly is wonderful! So
wonderful!

Fire Within

It came to me in the night, a thought from heaven above.
I sat there for years taking the pain of love.
I was in a trance on the issue of the words said about me.
It was not true as I was judged by them that were supposed
to be good.
I wondered from time to time what God thought of all this.
I woke up in the mornings sad.
I went to work with evidence in my heart that they were
holding me back.
I came home and it was true that they desired me dead.
I lived all those years hoping that it got better.
I went through all those years believing their lies as they told
it to me.
At the end, I finally took a stand and departed myself from
them.
So sad, that God is so displeased with us. I have this fire
within.

In a Moment's Time

The flow comes in as smooth as it can be.
The clouds cover me as a blanket with such heaviness.
As the rain comes down, the still is no longer there.
The earth screams its anger at me as I lay here.
My eyes cannot open as I am in total heaviness.
My mouth is closed by the loose earth.
I wonder as I lay here, what is next for me.
I was told that a person's life flashes by.
I wonder in a moment's time.

The Days of Time Came

I have been torn and bruised by the lies said of me.
I came to the sense of disgust as I have been in sadness.
The years came and went as I attempted to stay true to this
hypocrisy.
Yet, as the water drips on my life, my soul has become
closed to the unjust lies
of who I am. I was a man that came to God for refuge and
salvation. As the
years went by, the very ones that said that God lived in them
have destroyed my
life. I was once with them that claimed God.
I was once with them that claimed they were true to Him that
stands above all.
Yet, in all of those years I saw that they lived a lie. They
never were true to Him
that is above all. So I see and understand on this day that I
have to depart from
that allegiance that I took on that once upon a time. The days
came by to me
and went by to them. Today I am looked upon as this man
that lies have
created. So on this day that man came to life to be in a dark
world. I stand
before God as wrong as I could ever be. I stand before God
as right as I was
supposed to be. The days of time came.

About Her

I want the world to know how special she was.
My sister was an amazing person.
She was very unique in her own ways.
She spoke to me about a woman that suffered a lot
throughout her life.
She always told me that her children brought out the best in
her.
She loved her water with oatmeal in it.
She loved to watch the black and white movies.
She was unique in that she always loved her children.
She had a passion for them.
Her passion for her children was strong.
I remember when she would talk about our father. How she
would break
down crying. My sister loved God and she would always
thank God.
In her last few months on earth, I had the privilege to spend a
lot of time with
her. My sister had faith that she would get better so that she
could be with her
children. In her death bed, people from all over, all walks of
life came to see her and tell her that she was loved. On that
day, she was honored by everyone. For God even allowed
her enemies to come to be at peace with her.
She was a unique woman here on earth.
She left behind five children. My heart is broken to know
that
she suffered while the disease consumed her. I hated to see
her go
through that pain and suffering. When she passed away to be

with the lord, her children, grand children, family and friends were by her side. I remember her favorite pet, princes, a dog, crying missing her. She was a unique woman here on earth. Her daughters and sons miss her a lot. Her grandchildren remember her always. As for me, my sisters and my brothers, we love her always. It is amazing at the kind of person she was here on earth. I just thought that now that she is with my earthly father
in heaven, I can say that I look forward to see them again. I look around at all
that life brings, and sees that what matters is to love one another with no conditions.
Mayda spoke to me about the difference between life and living. My
sister was an amazing person. Life she said was a long road full of bumps and
pot holes. Living was getting through that road no matter the conditions it was under. She said that her children were unique to her. She said that God blessed her with
them and that she did not regret anything about them. I truly saw my sister in
the last few hours tell us a story about her. She was a unique person here on
earth.

Paradise

So fine like paradise is what I see.
I walk into that place where lovers go to love.
It feels, as if I am in a trance.
That woman that I seek is in this place.
I traveled from long distance in search for her.
Her beauty is strong like the sun.
One stare into her mysterious eyes and I get caught.
So I ask all over the world where can I find this woman.
Everyone is telling me that she is at the paradise place where
lovers go to love.
I am here. I am here. I am here.
Then finally I step into paradise.
There, just over the valley of earth's most beautiful creatures.
She stands tall, playing the harp, singing a morning song.
Her voice is enchanting. Her voice is smooth. Her beauty is
unforgettable.
As she finishes she walks towards me and she sees me with
tears of love.
I have traveled through time to see you. I stand here today to
let you know that
I am in love with you. In this place of Paradise I see you. In
this place of
paradise I rest with you. Take me here and do not let me go,
my lady of beauty and my lady of unforgettable presence.
There is no woman like you. Even in this place of paradise,
this is no ordinary love. I echo the love that I have for you
through the walls of this place called paradise. I believe in
your love. I believe in your beauty. I believe in your not so
ordinary love. Truly I stand in this place of paradise with
you.

The Reason for the Way

Dreams are born by unexpected people with the heart of a lion.

The sure way to fail in life is by not trying.

Action is the key ingredient to a successful mind.

Faith in yourself is the hardest convincing thing for you.

A few peoples' effort in the world can change a nation.

Think of yourself as a giant and a mighty warrior and you will be just that.

I am the best, I am one of a kind, and I am a doer and not a talker. My actions
speak for themselves. Dare me to succeed, and I will dare you to follow.

I am a special person in this world, with a special gift in this world, to help others to
be a success. Come and join my world and you will not regret it. We are one of a
kind. It started with me, then two, and now millions. We are the best.

Remember

I remember the way I was.

For many years my soul was full of his fire.

I remember the days of total stillness before Him.

Oh, I remember the days where the conversion took place.

I remember every single moment of fire that came from heaven above.

I remember when even the angels visited with messages from Him.

I remember dancing with his joy.

I, remember how I walked everyday talking to Him and how He answered me back.

I remember everything as if it was yesterday.

Lord, forgive me for all the things that I have done and not done.

Forgive me lord as I never have forgotten about you.

Remember me on my last day here on earth, that I may walk into heaven to be able to touch you and admire your wonderful presence. I remember all that I was and all that I am with Him. Thank you for everything as I am so grateful to you. I remember it all!

The Walk of Life

A moment was then when I was.
It all came to the end of that day.
Oh, so much death.
Oh, so much life.
I stood there on that day.
As the messenger delivered the message to me, I saw the fire
in the air.
I walked day in and day out.
Once or maybe twice, I saw the maker over him.
That time as I walked by the wall of death, I saw both of
them.
One looked gentle, and the other looked ravaged.
I thought to myself as I walked, who cares about what is
going on.
The winds are stronger and the clouds are darkened.
Who knows what is really going on?
Is this the day where it all comes crashing down to its end?
Ah yes, the walk of life.

Love for Him

The moment of time arrives for me.
Every morning I talk to him.
Yet all day and all night he talks to me.
While I am busy walking on this earth.
He has time to be with me.
While I get persecuted by my own kind in this land, he
always protects me and
provides me with shelter. When I came face to face with
death, he stepped in
the middle of our confrontation. As I saw the tough days in
my path, he brought
joy and peace to my life. I stand here now face to face with
the good lord.
As I take my place in his presence, and I say good bye to the
world of old, I truly
see that he has no time in his path, I truly see that he has no
pain, for he
endured it on the cross. He has a splendor look as he stands
in front of me. I
now see the love that he has for us on this earth.
Truly he is the Lord God.

A Change

Our beloved Nation of North America.
Tonight I got to see history.
History that has taken a new meaning.
A country that has been hurt and felt abandoned.
Has taken history by its arms.
Has taken a new way for the people.
As we as a Nation have spoken equality, and freedom for all.
Tonight I saw with my own eyes, that encryption come true.
Not so much in hate or in anger, but I saw McCain distribute
his wishes and
services, to a man that bears the color not seen as a President.
I saw the greatness of this country, the goodness of the
people, the decency of
politics, and the unity of many, bring back this nation to its
place of glory and
honor. Tonight, I saw a moment that my father whom fought
for this country
would off wanted to see. I saw tonight in this country, a
moment in history that
will live forever in infamy. I can only pray to our good
lord, that our future citizens would know that we saw
history being made. As Malcolm X, Martin Luther King,
and the many others, that would off thought, dreamed and
envisioned. I saw tonight a great move towards the next level
in a democratic society. I saw tonight the Constitution of this
nation come alive. A change I saw tonight.
November, 4, 2008 President Elect

A Heavenly Moment

I was at the bottom of the body of water.
I could not stand on the watery sand.
My heart felt blown as I pushed with my feet.
The muscles in my legs became weak.
As I looked up to the surface, I saw that great vision.
He stood at the right hand of His father and all of His glory.
Then I rose to the top of the body of water.
Then I knew I had a heavenly moment.

Give Me

give me your eyes to look
give me your beautiful face to stare
give me your lips so that I may kiss them deep
give me your intelligence so that I may learn from you
give me, give me your body so that I may sculpt it in my
heart
give me a moment and it will last a life time

The End of the Road with Dead Flowers

The road is narrow at the end
Its surroundings are evil and cry for revenge
The light over the hill is bright
I can touch the darkness from where I am
Oh the light is deep into the horizon
I can get there I can get there
The road is so long and dark
The way is so scary
But the road has dead flowers on its side
At the end when the light is nearest
The dead flowers are there waiting
Waiting as if they are waiting for me

Dear Puerto Rico

I sing onto you a song of love.
From your son from where I am.
Oh dear Borinquen, Mother of my family I sing.
As I listen to your Christmas songs, I think of you.
I dance the night away thinking of you.
Day and night my time is in your beauty.
The valleys and the bodies of waters show all that beauty is.
God truly exists, as I see his hand prints all over you.
I am one of your sons that have been far away thinking of
you as I sing this song of love. When I get off that plane and
touch the ground of Puerto Rico, my heart
beats with emotion. I am a writer, I am a poet, but today I am
a singer singing
onto you this love song. Every Christmas when I listen to my
brothers and sisters
sing Puerto Rican Christmas carols I cannot help but to cry. I
am attracted to
your beauty that shines so great in the Caribbean's.
Hug me today, lead me to the beaches of your body, dance
with me in your
valleys, feed me your great cuisines, and take my poetry that
I sing onto you. On
this night and on this day I am blessed with your thoughts. I
write to you about
the love that I have for you.

Same

Today, tomorrow, and everyday will be the same as yesterday
Everyday I hope and pray that those things would be
different in a way
As I wait for my day to start
I think of my lonely heart
The pain and suffering is come to see
it only brings me
to wish that someday I could be free
I wish there was a world for me
where I can laugh and sing
and everybody would just let me be
Today, tomorrow and everyday
will be same as yesterday
The same for this, the same for that
but especially the same for my lonely
heart

On the Operating Table

I was at the operating table and a lady approached me.
Hello fellow Christian friend,
In God we live and move and have our being.
We can do nothing without Christ.
Jesus is the way the truth and life.
For God so love the world he gave his only son Jesus.
Keep the faith.
Trust God's love and power.
Jesus — our
-Savior
-Redeemer
-Healer
-Provider
-Supplier
-Way maker
-Strength
Jehovah
Peace joy our all in all he will never fail us.

*I was coming out of an operation and when I looked around
the recovery room a lady was there to deliver a message
from God, reminding me that he is always with me. Then I
looked in front of me and another lady whom just came out
of surgery asked me, are you a Christian? I said "yes" then
she also confirmed this same message. Before I went into
surgery, I felt alone, and discouraged. God was there all
along protecting me and attending to me. Thank you Lord!*

Operator out of Control

Code name: Wizetry.
Now as I see myself on these chains of sorrow and pain, I think of how others thought that we were the untouchables when in reality we were the unbearable.
The *death dealers* were here.

The Anatomy of Hate

It comes from the many paths of hate.
It stood since the beginning of time as the evil one.
The envy came across the glamour of the other master's
vesture.
It was dark all over the world as it was written by Him.
The master of hate swelled on his own pride.
He thought of Him as the master sat on the throne.
His eyes were darkened.
His speech was impaired.
His clothes were stained.
His instruments to play the delight of the day for him had
broken.
All along as he stood in front of heaven's gate with his army
of fallen
degenerates, the master showed the world the anatomy of
hate that came from
that son of his. Suddenly, it was done.
He was cast to the world with his unholy anatomy.
Since then he has broken the arrow of hate.

Get Away

Got away from here.
Got online.
When shopping for tickets.
Took the flight with my wife.
Got off the plane.
Got in the car.
Drove to that place of paradise.
Walked the beach.
Swam the waters there.
Ate the food.
Looked at the sky full of stars.
All I said was "Boquerón you are the place here on earth".

Tranquility of the Sparrow

Puerto Rico is beautiful.
The tranquility here is special.
As I am sitting from the balcony I can actually here the earth
speak to me.
We are missing out for sure. I cannot even tell where the
ocean and the blue sky
meet. They are both like glass on this Caribbean floor.
The tranquility is accompanied by the beauty of this place.
The sun meets the sky, and the sky meets with the ocean to
dress in beautiful
attire. In the mornings the green earth stands still, while the
sky just hovers over
its sister the ocean. The sun looks at me as if I am one of its
children that are
lost. Then when I am well aware, the moon lets me sleep
under its cuddly arms.
I think to myself over and over again, perhaps I should be
here and not there.
This is a place where the tranquility is like a sparrow.

I Caught the Wind

It is said at times that the still of life is a moment that passes
by.
It is said that the moment that lasts an eternity is the moment
caught in a
photograph.
It is said that a life's long journey is in being in the arms of a
troubled soul.
This is what was said, what is said, and what is to be said.
I caught the wind of time here on this day.
I caught the wind.

Storm of Wonder

The path of wind came through life today.
Yet as the wind was raving through the blessings that I had
received, it was a
war of spirits in the air. The storm raged with a fury as if it
wanted to destroy my
very being. I stood there in the middle of that whirlwind
while the storm and its
fury yelled my name. It was a hate call as it whirled back and
forth. But I stood
there looking at the storm and its hate. We stared down at
each other for the
many hours that the storm pounded my life. I heard all of its
hate and I saw all
of its malice. As I spent more time in front of this storm
staring at its fury the
smaller he was becoming to me. Then in a split of a moment,
the storm's fury
ended and became nothing. Just like that it was over.

The Rage of Garandeget

The battle was strong at the hills of Galbothia.

The King and his son stood side by side in power.

The battle grew in their favor as the Emerald guards fought valiantly.

The elves of the territory of Galbothia stood at the highest peak of the hills.

The enemy came from all fronts of the war zone.

Yet it came to be that the last charge was called.

Then as the King charged with his mighty army, the enemy stood still for the

slaughter.

It was then that the rage of Garandeget showed itself.

A dragon, that came from the hills of the country.

With one swoop, then a second pass, and a third, it was over.

He made his presence known and the enemy was defeated.

The rage was strong and swift.

Off with the enemy's strength, so it was done.

The battle was over.

The Way of Truth

He stood over my life showing me the way.
As it came to be a strong point of salvation, he came to me.
Was there ever a difference in the eternal life?
I asked myself that question as I went about my business.
God who are you?
Lord can you really save me?
Then out of the wind came a moment of truth.
The way that was written in the book of life, he is.
So he came to me and gave to me the miracle of life.
It came as the way of truth.

The Creatures *Gigalets*

In the land of Gammon the creatures Gigalets live.
They stand about five feet tall, with green hair, big eyes that
are yellowish with
ears that are pointy. When a Gigalet is born he is born at the
age of one
hundred years of age. The incredible creature ages
backwards. As he ages
backwards he goes through adolescent stages.
Amazingly, his abilities become diminished as he age
decreases. At his end
when the creature Gigalet reaches the age of one. He
transforms into a
Mentesar. A beautiful flying bird that has a yellow eye in the
middle of his head,
has wings that are of rainbow colors, and a singing bird noise
that is pleasant to
a person's ears. A magnificent transformation this Gigalet
performs as he
reaches his last stage.

Count Bizen

A black velvet robe he wears to the parade.
Circling the depths of the no good of this world he goes.
Striking every missed fortuned life he is.
As the count Bizen releases his power over the village.
Help is requested by the residents.
The moon strikes the night hours.
The count is once again on the move to do his will.
Yet a shout of despair is heard by the villagers.
Then suddenly a cry of misfortune echoes across the hills.
A sudden silence dwells in the midnight hour.
Bizen has come across the creature that he never wanted to meet.
A man full of God's mighty power has met with this Bizen.
Yet, with one word from his faith, Bizen is stricken forever.
It is now over. Back to the world's grave he goes.

Reason

I want the world to know about the goodness that exists in God. There have been moments in my life that I have been ill and God has healed me. There have been moments where I have felt alone to the point where all I could do is cry out to God and he has sent friends to my life. When I gave my life to the lord and he was cleaning my body out of the junk of the world and I was shaking and wanting to have the things of the world inside of me. God purified me and kept me away from the temptation of the world. When I went to face my old enemies to let them know that I was not going back to the old life that I had, God touched them and they had mercy on me. When I needed money and clothes because I had nothing God showed favor over me and got me work and provided what I needed in my life. When I requested from God that my family would hear the good Lord's voice, God's presence and word came to them and they responded. I am proof that the Lord is real and that he is the reason for life itself. I love you God.

Never Ending Thought

I never thought missing someone would be so difficult to deal with. As I wake I stand next to my shield in sorrow and pain. As I walk in the heat of the day, I feel torn and bruised. My heart is visible to my enemies and my loved ones. Now, as I head to battle, to stand for the last time against our mortal enemy. I feel the loneliness in my heart. My lady the Queen, said farewell to me as I left to the battle field with the army of Galbothia. My son looked at me deep into my eyes without speaking, weeping in his heart with great pride as I was not to come back. I am a blade fighter from Galbothia, the few of men that are raised to show no fear, and to fight for the freedom of our people. As I walk with my shield and my sword by my side, I stare into the paradise scenery of my country. Now at the edge of the gates of Molden, we see the darkness that our enemy has brought to our world. It is then that I realize that there is no room for selfishness. There is no room for fear. There is no room for weakness. Into battle I go with my men and my army. Into this dark battle for survival we go. We are the last of the blade fighters of Galbothia.

By the Sea

The entry was long and short as life intended to give. The beauty of a woman passed my way to be. I stood at mount victory with my shield and sword. Then my armor met me as she came to me. A Knight I stood and a King I was. She said with her eyes all that was to be said. Then I stood there on my horse to see, to see her beauty go back to the lilies by the sea.

Continue as Friends

As a child I saw u as an elder through your height and not
your age.
As we parted ways to begin our journeys we found out how
our lives and memories would never fade.
Though now time has passed, and life surpassed our destiny.
It held within itself to always stay as friends.

The Crusader from Time through Time

A most serene day is at hand.
Yet tomorrow seems so tempting.
So when I took a step towards that.
Why then did life hold back?
At night I see the stars but,
I wonder do the stars see me?
I walk on the sand at the beach.
Yet I wonder does the sand know that I am walking on it?
At night, when I am writing my lyrics of life,
I feel the pain it provides.
Yet, I wonder have I caused pain to others in this life?
Because at the end when it is all said and done,
I will find out like everyone else has found out.
That God has already been there and knows all that was
done.
Yet I often wondered how I would be leaving this earth?
Now at this moment, all that I have done and all that I have
seen and
all that I have been through, has come back to see me at a
glance.
Now, all I have to say is.
It was fun while I was alive.

Twilight Traveler

So you must wonder from time to time.
A twilight traveler stopped bye.
He stood there at this place of solitude.
The world breathes pain and loveless moments on us all.
Yet the answer lies so clear from up above.
God sends his love to us all.
The truth goes further to show us all.
How we too can be a friend to the end with love.

Beauty Cursed

From the corridors of the world I saw her walking. As she approached me I saw
her beauty. With her height she astonished my thought of her elegant posture.
She got closer than ever before, and I gazed at her beautiful hair. She reminded
me of a sapphire stone with a special glare of the beauty hidden beneath the
earth. I gazed at her lips and they were unique. The skin on her body was fair
and beautiful. But at that moment in time that had stopped. Her eyes have
hidden wonders. Her eyes have hidden beauty. Her eyes have the past, present
and future. The world looks for beauty in her eyes. I got lost on that day when I
peaked into her eyes. I was shocked when I saw the beauty that she possessed.
I am now trapped, caged in her beauty that haunts me with her eyes. Yours
forever, twilight traveler.

Faith Shown, Faith Not Shown

The way to show that you have faith in yourself is better
demonstrated by
leaving a trail of evidence, that no matter what happens, has
happened or is
going to happen. You have gotten it done. Leave a trail of
proof in your life.

The King and Lady Aline

I foresaw a shadow in the forest as I raced to the front of the river. Its mouth was swelling with glory. But the shadow in the forest would follow me still. I looked and I looked. I saw and I saw. I stood there on that cliff as she worked her art by the side of that river. She was fascinating. She was tall and her eyes were glowing from afar. Her body was slim and unique. I could not hear her talk but I felt her heart beat. I knew as my king sent me on this quest, to seek for the Lady Aline. She was the woman that took art from his Kingdom. She was the woman who took his heart when she left on her quest for the highest level of her calling. I have found her. She is there, she is here, and she will be home soon my King. Lady Aline.

A Site in the Day

I was at the edge of life
as day came to end the night.
I stayed to the burning of the sun.
At that moment I saw her walking by me.
On that morning I fell for her beauty.
I am a nocturnal creature.
I am a lover of the night.
But her beauty is like no other.
I saw this woman across the fields of love.
The Sun burns my skin and my life.
Yet I am willing to risk seen her and know her as a true love.
I can describe her eloquently, her curly hair, her fair skin, and
her eyes that I can stare into and get lost in them.
Her lips are magical the way they look.
Her body is unique as that of a Queen.
I finally met her on a pleasured night.
We crossed paths by an alley to club Lasers.
I showed myself to her while dressed in black and with my
darkened eyes.
I introduced myself to her and she spoke her name to me.
Then I stared at her deep colored eyes.
Suddenly, she was still for the chilled bite.
I went for her neck and her thriving skin.
She then stopped me with a sudden halt.
It was then that I found out that she was a day walker.
She was one of a kind, a site in the Day.

The Night Came. The Night Went

The night whispers moments of sensuality while the day speaks of its best moments. Yet the energy from ones body ravages the moment into another dimension. The night is always mysterious and unique. The night came. The night went.

In The Still of The Day, The Mood Haunts Me

Still, on a sitting position I am.
A breeze comes in through the doors of my heart.
As I reflect on my troubled past.
My life settles me hard on this day.
My tears are tears within my heart.
So, I ask myself, where did I go badly?
Suddenly, out of the sky it came,
a fortune of love to settle my day.
I look around at my dear family's way.
Too see that I am blessed beyond today.
My heart hurts as my life trembles.
My love inside is so strong for someone even as the day ends
with no love.
I am me and that is how I am. My hurt is temporary and my
love is true.
All I can say is that today I sit still remembering the days.
Tomorrow I look forward to become better than today.
I am in love. My life is pure. I love with my heart wounded
no more.
In the still of the day, the mood haunts me.

A Picture and Its Presence

The movement of life always stands still in a picture. Neither
time nor life, have
anything to say there. But the picture reveals total stillness of
time. A
magnificent analogy through a *lens*.

Remembering

Perhaps time came and time went. Perhaps the shadows of
life were real on that
day. Maybe love can stand still for a moment. The Sun rose
on that day. The
Sun wrapped its arms around him, as the world new the
brother, we had. As the
world new the father he was. Today we stand here letting you
know. That we all
miss you since you let go. There was only one Carlos as far
as I know. But there
was only one brother that we six knew? We miss your way of
life as you cruised
on that road. We remember today the man you were. We love
you and
remember you on this day that is so gloomy and dull. We
know you
danced, sang and play the music from your heart. Oh, how
lovely it is to
remember you so.

True Love Comes From Inside

So much inside that, I cannot escape the arms of her warmth.
So deep
inside that in the darkest moments of this life, I feel the hope
from her love.
Can you imagine, the deepest of love coming across the
deepest of
desires. For once, she is my love and I am hers. She extends
the greatest in
me. She brings out the best out of my life. I am forever truly
in debt to her
love that comes from another world. The ultimate lover
versus the ultimate
love.

To Seek and Not To Be Forgotten

The pearl of the realm of sands runs deep into the core of
souls. Can the beat of
the heart speaks for itself? Was there ever a question at how
awesome his
presence was. Was there ever a moment of forgiveness
without a moment of
repentance? The road of souls has narrowed itself on these
last days. The path
of the righteous has become extinct in this world. Maybe,
just maybe the coming
of the Lord came and went. Maybe it's just the evil of men
that has caused
the world to go on a rampage?

My Moment of Speed

I just drive day and night. I drive. Nothing like driving a Benz! With the satellite
radio on and feeling the heart beat of a V 8 CLS Engine. I write my greatest
works in these vehicles. Just my cars and our guest, the music from my
I-pod. I am astonished at the feeling this machine brings to my presence. I am
captivated by her look. She feels my heart. She sees my pain. She even makes
me wonder as I drive through the streets of New York. Oh my, Alphabet City, all
its magic, and wonders. I am astonished. I am amazed. I am in a trance. No
wonder. No wonder I am from another realm. Are there any others like me here
on earth? I will keep searching and searching for more. I live day by day, with
focus, and commitment. Can you feel the love it brings to your heart? Listen to
her purr as a kitten purrs. Fascinating at the impact she pulls at the light. Look at
her and her beauty. She is majestic. She is a sapphire in the midst of stones. A
delightful presence she has. Then again she is called Mercedes.

In Our Dreams

In a time that time forgot. That was you and me. We used to get lost in
our dreams. Our love had no boundaries. We made love everywhere, even in our
dreams. The moments that we had were unforgettable. It was a time that it
did not exist on earth but in our kind of life it did. It lived and lived again. We
were strangers to nothing? Day in and day out we were lovers of each other. I
cannot ever forget of them moments of love. A fallen Angel I became and a
fallen lover to you I was. We used to get lost in our dreams.

The Radiant Man

Time is for you and me. If you must love a woman, love her
as an ultimate lover.
If you must fight, fight as a warrior from the past. If you
must live life, live life to
the fullest. If you must talk, put action behind your words. At
the end that is
what will be remembered from you and me. See you on the
other
side. You know who you are.

Let Us Do It Again

There is only one way to do that. The attraction goes every which way. The moment has passed but the time has come. Again desires came and went. As the night left, so did we. It was wild and wild and wild again. But then again only you can and you can and you too can. It was an experience. Yes, a pleasant one we must admit. Then again it is not like it has not happened before. Life is good! See you Friday night, same place different time!

At Times It Is Just Us!

Sometimes in life one must let go to
get back. One must war to battle a
fight. One must dislike, too learn to
like. One must give so that it can be
taken even more. One must love
short lived so that true love can
evolve. One must kick some tail in
and out so that one is understood.
One must stay the course inside and
not out side. One must look in the
mirror so that the mirror can
show you only you. At the end when all
is said and done. One must know that
it was good here on earth and that
the time has come. All in a days work!

Race through Time

I raced through time to seek and to want. I reached the edge of life not once but twice. I met her by that time at the portal of space. She was an amazing woman. She robbed me of my peace and my stability in my mind. She took my heart and gave it life again. Again and again, I raced through time. That woman named Brenda took it to my life. She was once a princess in that domain of love. Now she reigns as a queen in a castle of loveless souls. It is I, a Knight from a distanced traveled road that seeks to secure her love within a heart. It is a race through time.

The Night Was My Best Friend

As I encountered the feelings of the Night,
I became a soul of Despair.
I felt even amongst the truest of love, a vessel of emptiness.
There while taking it all in over a drink of what many called
relaxation.
I encountered a new friend.
She was amazing.
As the lights were on me,
as the excitement was all around the room.
I was welcomed like a lost child searching.
It was amazing to find and see others like me.
Dancing the night, and talking about the worries of the day to
each other.
Accepting ones way of life and not ignoring others existence,
that is what I saw.
I was in a trance last night.
She took me into her arms and made me a part of the night.
I felt released for the first time in a long time.
I went all night with her.
She never departed from me.
She was a unique entity.
Then I departed from her.
The sun came out.
The day arrived.
My joy had ended at that moment.
I said goodbye to her.
I kissed her.
I waved to her as it came to an end.
She was my best friend.

A Fantasy with Her

He picks her up in his car. They drove to lovers point. There
at that hill they indulge in a forbidden conversation. While
the sun is rising he grabs her hair and tilts her head back. He
then kisses her neck. While she asks for more, he lifts her
up and places her on the hood of his Red Corvette. There he
slips his hand under her skirt and she knows at that moment
that he is near. She roles her eyes back as if welcoming this
moment of seduction. Suddenly, she unbuckles his belt. After
he positions her legs on a comfortable position, he starts
his sexual ingestion. As they are making love the sun hides
and the clouds appear. Unexpectedly, the rain starts to fall. At
that moment they are both out of control in their love making
moment. Once they reach the end of their love moment,
they realize one thing. They have made love under the sun
and under the rain. It was an incredible experience.

Since The First Time

Moving on with the best, I choose you my love. Always you. There is none other but you. You are the woman of my dreams. Ever since the beginning it is been you. I am in a trance as I look at your beauty. You had me since the beginning. It is just us two. All us! You are a body of wonders, a mystery to be loved by me. You are you and that is what I love about you. Come let us leave this place and let the magic start. Love at all time. We desire each other at every moment. Since the first time!

Lost the Will to Love

He lost the will. He walks the earth. He stood beside his
thoughts of you. Day and night it did not matter. This man is
from this world. He has lost the will to love. He has lost the
will to love you. He doesn't like this place at all. It makes
him wonder what it's all about. He never wanted to be your
friend. He wanted to be your lover. He wonders to and from
on this earth. He moves on. He has lost the will to love. He
asks to be taken away, away by the waves of life's most
hurtful moments. He did not want to be your friend. He did
not want to be here and there any longer. He has lost the
will to love over and over again. He has left the shadows of
love once and for all. Now he drifts again on earth to pursue
a love that once was. He has lost the will to love. Hear his
footsteps as he nears your heart. You cannot see him. You
remember him, you remember what it could off been. It is
deeper than what it was seen by your mind. An ultimate
lover has fallen short of such glory. He was deeper than what
your mind showed you. He never wanted to be your friend.
He wanted to be your lover. He never wanted to place you
there on that wall. He loved you deeply with the desires of a
man. He placed you on that moment as he handled you that
night. He was a lover that came across your path. He caused
the greatest love making moment. He said it was magical
the night full of sexuality between the two of you. He never
wanted to be just your friend. He now drifts on to the next
level of his walk on this earth. He was he and he chose you
amongst many. The beauty of a soul without love, and the
beauty of a soul that has love, that is you. It is amazing
how he defined his moments with you, woman of pleasure,
woman of beauty, and woman of mystery. He was turned on

by you. He was out of breath with you. Remember? Some never reach that breathless love making moment. Yet he mastered it with you. He recorded it all for memories of time. Now he moves on, walking on this earth in search of a love that can surpass you. He lost the will once. He lost his will once to love you.

Never Enough

I try to give it all to you. I try. But it is never enough, never. You are driving me crazy. You are making me nuts. Can you stop? Stop your doing. Let go of me. Come on baby. Stop it. Be kind, and have mercy. You are just too much woman of seduction. Get a grip on yourself. Tomorrow is another day. Don't you think?

Friday

You should of never have come into my domain. I knew this was going to happen. Yes it is good I know. It is awesome. I mean, the night was long. Yes it was. All night long. I could understand that. But I must move on now. Call me before you know it. It will be Friday again. We can hook up. That is right. Have an adventure of a night or day. Don't matter to me. I travel for the time. I move for the moment. I do what feels good. Yes I am yours. You are right. Don't mind me and my ways. I look at life in a different way. You liked that hu? Ha, ha, ok. I got some more for you. Don't worry. But remember Friday is your time. Not Saturday, Sunday, Monday, Tuesday, Wednesday, or Thursday. Friday! All about you on Friday dear! See you later. I must go now.

I Could Count On You

I love waking up in the morning. I realize that you are awesome. I love in the mornings, to talk to you. You listen so closely. My words to you are so real. You never judge me, even though you can. It is amazing at your patience with me. I truly appreciate your time. I know I am not perfect. I know I failed at life. I know yet that I could count on you. Thank you father for being there! Your Son, Me!

In Love with Life

I'm so in love with life. I look at the sky and I am in amazement. I look at the mountains as I drive my car. I see his finger prints of his art all over it. I gaze at the sun and I am blinded by its beauty and power. Then I see you in my mind. I remember you. I am pleased with your beauty. You touched my heart my friend. I am thankful for that. My heart has you in it. Just like all the other things that make my life. I am in love with life!

Short Stories

Demons Visited, as Angels Visited

On October 25, 1990 he was outside of a night club called Yesterday's café. Raven waited there for a friend of his that was supposed to meet him outside at the parking lot. He waited as the clock turned to two in the morning on a cold Friday. Suddenly, a man with a wicked tongue walked towards Raven. Dressed in a black velvet suit he stood in front of Raven. Quickly Raven reached for his gun but the wicked tongued man looked at him and paralyzed his hands. He then looked at him again and paralyzed his legs. The wicked looking man stood there as he spoke to Raven and told him that he had a message for him. Then as the wicked man was standing he placed his hands into his chest and pulled out a sword with blue watery flames on it. As he held the sword and aimed it at Raven; Raven thought that he was going to die. The wicked man kept on judging Raven and tormenting his soul with tongues that were unknown. At one point, the man closed his eyes and he struck Raven with all of his anger and hate. Raven could not move at all. Even when Raven attempted to call for help, he was not able to. Raven's tongue had a sap of some sort that was color black and had the smell of a dead person. Once again the wicked man closed his eyes to continue to torment Raven's heart. As Raven had his eyes closed he saw people in a place of fire and brimstone. He saw the unthinkable as people were eating other people alive. He was standing there waiting as the wicked man had Raven paralyzed to the point that he could not breathe. As the wicked man walked towards Raven, the sword with blue fire was poking Raven. Raven saw the drips of his own blood coming down from the side of his arms. Raven saw the wicked man laughing at him as he tortured him. It was then at that moment that another man appeared. That man was dressed in a blue jacket, with black pants, and black shoes as with an angelic look. As the other man approached Raven, the wicked man placed Raven in deeper bondage. Raven could hear the growls coming out of that wicked man that was hurting him. Raven heard the wicked man growling like a cat full of rage. The wicked man suddenly pointed to the ground and black shadows appeared by his side. The wicked man called on demons to be present to fight the other man that had appeared as an Angelic being. As the wicked man and the demons got ready to strike the Angelic looking man, a light of gold color appeared. Suddenly there were two other Angelic men standing by Raven. The wicked men had blue swords that had watery blue fire on it. As the men moved their swords, the blue watery fire moved with them. Then each one of them started to strike the Angelic men fire swords. As each sword clashed with each other, the lightning bolts were bright and yellowish. They went back and forth striking each other. The growls came loud from the wicked demon men. Suddenly the battle was over and the Angels approached Raven. Raven became frightened as one of the Angelic men spoke to him. The Angelic man did not move his lips at all. Raven was able to understand the Angel's language as he spoke with his mind. Raven could hear and understand everything that the Angel was telling him. Then one Angel said to Raven that their names were Gremeda, Gormetha, and Luxtrousa. He said that they were the Angels of night and the Angels of day. The Angels stood maybe ten to fifteen feet tall. As he touched Raven with his hand all of his wounds were healed, his tears were gone and he could move again. Gormetha said to Raven that God had sent them to protect him as the demon of anger and his servants of hate were after Raven's soul. The Angel also told Raven that he was to go and play softball with some men that

God was going to put in his path. A few days later Raven found himself attending a church service. There he heard the same voices and when he looked down towards the altar area where the Pastor was preaching. The voice told Raven that he was to listen for instruction about the task that God had given him. He was to be with the softball players and open his own heart to them. The voice said, "In your heart Raven they shall find my Son" then Raven woke up. It was an experience that he never forgot.

The Crossing of the Swords

You lift me up as a leaf from the ground. I feel no weight in my body. I am high off the ground at an altitude that I never thought existed. Oh, I see the stars next to me. I actually feel the rays from the sun touching me. I have to laugh and laugh at how mighty is your presence. What is this? Here comes a person walking towards me. He approaches me dressed in white clothing. Who is this man? I am going to stand still on this ground of gold and wait for him. Now he is here looking at me and asks me with his eyes to follow him. I have to laugh because his lips never moved and I could hear him talk. I laugh even more because I answer him without moving my lips and he hears me. I answered him to lead the way. Ok, here we go into this purple, blue, white, gold, and yellow cloud. As we walk I see a huge wall from across the galaxy. I am at awe to see this as we walk on space, or on air, or on something. I laugh again because I am just so full of joy. The colors are so beautiful here in the heavens that we are walking on. As we walk this man points to the top of the huge wall. Yes, I see it. Yes, I do. I could actually see people flying near this gigantic wall. They look like people from what I can see. As we get nearer the wall I can hear voices full of joy. I feel as if I want to go over the huge wall to see what the commotion is all about. I look at this man that I am following and he is laughing full of joy. I feel such peace here in this place towards this great wall. As we walk this man points towards the wall and says for me to follow him towards the gates. I cannot stop laughing as we are walking on this ground colored gold. I am so much at peace and full of joy. As we walk I admire this man's attire. His clothing is colored white, blue and gold. Then again that is the colors that I can compare it to. His hair is shiny like a yellow leaf from a tree. Then I see his hair off the reflection of the sun to be like a pearl color making him young looking. I am excited to get to where we are going. I cannot wait to get there. As we walk we both are laughing full of joy. However, our lips and mouths are not moving, but we can hear each other talk. As we walk I look at my arms and I don't see my scars on my skin. So, I ask him, what happened to my skin? It is without any wrinkles and scars. He looks at me with his deep glossy eyes and his bright smile. That is good enough for me, as I am smiling as well. I want to get inside these walls. As I look up beyond the height of the walls, I see the giant bird looking creatures fly over us. Wow, I think to myself as we see these giant creatures fly over us. I count like twelve of them over us. He turns around and points towards them and says to me "look at their prayers." I reply, "I could see them penetrating the beautiful clouds." These colors are colors that I have never seen before. I am excited about this. Now I want to get inside faster and see what is going on inside. I finally ask him for his name. I want to know who you are Mr. He looks at me and says to me that he is the one that has been assigned to me since I was born. I ask, "What are you talking about Mr.?" We laugh over and over again as it seem so funny to me at what I am hearing. Wow, I feel so good here right now at this moment. This walk is awesome by these giant walls. As I continue to walk with my guide I see so many beautiful flowers and plants. The colors are mesmerizing to my mind. I stop and grab a flower and then I drop them on the ground and they grow back into the ground that looks like a cloud. I could not stop laughing at how much fun I am having. I reach to the ground and grab also some of this glittery dust that I see everywhere. I ask him "what is this dust that I see?" He tells me that the dust is cloud coloring mist that comes from the heavens above. I continue to follow him. As we are walking, I tap him on his shoulder and I ask him what are those giant things flying over us that have huge wings? He points towards them and tells me that they are the finest in their place. He also tells me that they are going to where I am going to live for eternity. He tells me that they are called Cherubims of the highest because they are appointed to high positions. At this moment, I am at peace. We are almost there. I can see the giant gates. They look blue with huge symbols of some sort. I wonder if once I go in; will, I ever come back out? He suddenly turns around and says to me that no one ever wants to leave this place. I ask him if he was assigned to me since I was born, then what is going to happen to me when I go into this heavenly place to live. He tells me with great joy that I will get to worship the sender uninterrupted for eternity. He also tells me that I will get to judge him of his duty on serving me on earth to the moment I go into heaven. Suddenly he looks at me and says with his mind, that not to worry that he will be in heaven with him. I stopped and I wonder if he gets placed to another person on earth. He turns his head and says no, his duty is complete once I go into heaven. I try to feel sad about this but I cannot. He says that for me not to worry because he will be in heaven there as well worshipping God. He also says that the glory belongs to God and God only. I smile at him and I tell him that I agree. I finally ask him for his name. He says that his name is Eglorium, Angel of the most highest. His name he says in heaven means attached to the Lord God. He then extends his right hand and we get lifted up in the air. I say to myself, Wow. The gates are there I say to him. He says yes there are the gates. Suddenly he says to me to wink my eyes, and when I wink, we arrive at the gates. The gates are gigantic. They remind me of two towers going into the clouds. As I stand in front of them I look straight up and I cannot see their end. It is amazing the beauty these gates have. They are covered with symbols, and two huge hands with rays of sun and colors coming out of the hands. I also see a book that is open being held by the two giant hands. I am amazed at the beauty of the gates. Well, I say to myself here we are and ready to walk through the gates. Just before we walk in I am going to ask him a few more questions. The Angel says "sure Edwin, go right ahead." I ask, "Where you the one?" The one that confronted my brother, my best friend, and me at the railroad tracks when we were teenagers. He replied "yes" I am the one. So I ask another question, "are you the same one that was at my house when the demons showed up and tried to hurt me?" I was only ten years old on that October evening in the bathroom of my house when that occurred. He replies again by saying "yes Edwin". So you were there also, when I wanted to commit suicide behind the elementary school. He replies "yes" to that question as well. You gave me a message from God that I never forgot. God said that he loves me always no matter what. You actually took the drugs and threw them in the sewer drainage at the yard of the school. I am now full of hope and wonder. I look at my hands suddenly and they are glowing. All around my body I have this glow of life around me. I look at Eglorium and he too has the glow of life. I ask, tell me Eglorium, "what is going to happen to my family and friends?" "What will happen to the kids that I know and the Church people?" He looks at me and tells me that not to worry because God is taking care of them all. He says that they will miss me, but they will know where I will be at waiting for them. I ask him about my wife and he says that she will shortly be with God as well. From where I am standing he points at the crowns of this new home that I have. He even tells me that some of my friends and family are there waiting for me. Wow I say to myself. I am excited about this. I actually can remember all of my friends and family. However, I cannot remember their names. He turns and says that in heaven we all have new names and the old names are no longer good. Amazing I tell myself. Before we go in Eglorium I want to thank you for everything. He smiles at me and says don't thank me and bring all the Glory to our God. He is waiting for you and me. He tells me that when we go inside we will stand in front of the good Lord. I tell Eglorium that I know him personally since I was twenty one years old when he saved me. I am greatly thankful to God for what he has done in my life. Suddenly from where I am standing, my whole life flashes by me as a bolt of lightning. I realize now with greater conviction that God's mercy, God's word, and love is greater than what anyone can ever imagine. I love him very much and I am happy to be here. I am ready Eglorium. Let us go through the gates and go inside. As we walk in I am approached by an Angel with a great glow. The ground I walk on is neither solid nor soft. The people in this heaven are all glowing and are all pure. We are walking towards this throne with yellow rays. As I walk towards God, Eglorium bows. Eglorium then says my name but I cannot understand it. I cannot even say it or even write it out. We finally go inside walking through the gates of heaven. I see the Angel glowing and in total worship. His vesture has changed to this pure white glow as did my own. When I look at Eglorium's eyes, they were white and blue. I could not help but to notice the millions of people here in this heaven. They are all smiling and with a look of joy. Suddenly, I see someone approaching me. That is my earthly father. He looks at me and points towards the throne. I say yes I will go there. It is nice to see my earthly father looking so young and so happy. Now it is me and the Angel walking there. All around us there are colors that I have never seen before. There are also, Angels and I see and hear different kinds of musical tunes full of harmony. I also see different kinds of colored trees. I am amazed at this beautiful place called heaven. We are getting closer and closer. My body feels elevated from the ground. As I am walking I can see a tree with rays coming out of it. The tree is gigantic as big as a mountain. On top of the tree, I see bird like creatures flying over singing to God. I look at Eglorium and he smiles at me. Our walk is a pleasant walk but I am floating on air it seems. I look at my feet and they are all colored white and clean. We are here. Tears of joy are in my eyes yet I cannot cry. I am so happy. I am so full of joy. There are these steps into the throne of God. The steps are made of a white stone that looks like water. I hear singing and praises all over heaven. I can even see the praises as I am walking into the Lord's throne. The praises are colorful. Yes, I can see the praises. Unbelievable, I am at awe as I see this place. The Angel asks me to walk into the throne of God. Just before we go in I bow my head. I cannot help to think about where God has taken me from. Everything is flashing by me as I bow before his great presence. When I was eight years old I remember being put in a bath tub with my brother, as my parents did Santerismo over us. I remember the blood of chickens being poured over our heads and naked bodies. I also remember while driving home from work just after midnight what had happened to me. I fell asleep at the wheel and my car went off the road; just when the car was going to go over a cliff by the bridge, I saw these two huge white hands grab the steering wheel of the car and steer the car back on the road. I remember the State Trooper that pulled me over, getting out of his patrol car and asked me where the other person in the car was. I also remember getting into a car accident and being unconscious as I heard God's voice. He said while I was unconscious "Edwin today is the day, come to me." I remember at how much fear I had when I heard his voice and knowing that I was dying. On that day my life changed. At this very instance, I remember clearly talking to thousands of people about Jesus. I even remember leading my earthly father to the Lord. As I bow my head before going into this throne, I remember my brother and me getting baptized at a church in Brookfield Connecticut. Many things are coming to my mind as I am going into God's throne. Now I see at how meaningful it all is. I try to cry but I cannot. The Angel tells me that in here there is no suffering and no crying. We are finally walking in. Here we go. As I am walking in I can only say to myself that I don't deserve to see this. I am totally at awe at the beauty of this throne. He is beautiful from all areas in this throne. He stands mighty on his throne. He is walking towards me. He is walking towards me. I look towards the Angel and he is no longer with me. God approaches me. He is holding a crown. He hugs me, and kisses me on the forehead. I don't know what to do. I am in total joy. He places the crown on my head in front of all of heaven's residents. The crown has writings on it "well done good and faithful servant". I immediately fall to his feet. I bow before him and I start to worship him. He suddenly lifts me up. As he does this I look into his eyes and they are as clear as pure water. I look at his hands and I see the marks from the nails from when he was crucified. I asked Jesus, "what do I do now?" Live forever my son, he says to me. He then introduces me to all of heaven, and even introduces me to the Cherubims. I see millions upon millions of saints in this heaven. I take the crown that he put on my head and I give it back to him. I tell him that he is the one that is worthy of a crown and of all the crowns. I tell him "you are my King, you are my all". I kneel before him and he is rejoicing with me and the others. As I am walking all of heaven is clapping and cheering. I see no enemies anywhere. I am truly home. Then suddenly I woke up laying on the couch in my living room.

Angel in Flight

June 12, 1991, a man by the name of Eddie took a flight to San Juan Puerto Rico. As he sat in his assigned seat he thought of many things. He felt empty inside and perhaps that was the reason he went to Puerto Rico searching for answers. Nevertheless, in this flight Eddie encounter the reality of life from an unusual person that was sent by God. This person sat in seat 19A at an American Airlines flight number 442. The flight was not full at all. To Eddie's right sat a woman that appeared to be in her mid forties'. To his left was a man that looked in his sixties and he was sleeping. The flight was bumpy as there was a lot of unusual turbulence announced by the Captain of the aircraft. Eddie looked to his right and he saw the lady staring at him. She said to him "don't be scare and don't be troubled by life's painful moments, because God is with you and has a purpose for your life." Eddie heard the message and was touched to the point that he was not frightened. Shortly after, he fell asleep for exactly one hour. After he woke up he looked for the lady that was sitting to his right. After listening to the Captain announcing the flight's destination, Eddie asked the flight attendant where the woman that sat on that seat went. The flight attendant told him that there was no one at that seat since the seat was empty. Eddie took a walk around the plane to see if he could find the woman. The woman was no where in the plane. After arriving to his destination, Eddie realized that an Angel visited him with a message from God.

Midnight Ride, Midnight Encounter

I was heading home at around twelve mid night on a Thursday. I had just completed a sixteen hour shift. I worked at a Correctional Facility in Cheshire Connecticut as a Correctional Officer. It was a cold November night or maybe I should say morning. Nevertheless, it was cold and I was tired. I got on I-84 east towards home. I fell in and out of sleep as I drove my car on the highway. Finally, while driving, I fell asleep and drove my car into the middle of the ditch grass area of the highway. As the car was about to go over the embankment off the bridge I opened my eyes. I saw two hands grab the steering wheel and I watched the car go back on the highway. Immediately, a State Trooper's cruiser lights appeared behind my car. I pulled over, and he approached my car. With my window down, he asked me for my driver's license and registration. He looked at my uniform and asked me where I was coming from. I told him that I was coming from the prison where I worked as a guard. He asked me if I was ok. I told him that I was very tired and sleepy. The Trooper walked around the rear of my car and with his flashlight looked at the back seat area of my car. He again came to the driver side of the car. He asked me if he could drop me off at home and leave my car on the side of the highway. I accepted the trooper's invitation and got into his cruiser. The truth is that I was afraid of what I had experience in my car. The two huge white hands that were driving my car made me afraid. As I was in the Trooper's car I could not help but to notice him staring at me. After five minutes in the vehicle the Trooper asked me. "Tell me one thing officer Rivera. Where did the other person that was in your car go when I pulled you over?" I replied, "I was alone." The trooper explained to me that I was not alone and that he saw another person next to me in the front seat. I told him that I had seen two hands grab the steering wheel, as I was ready to go over the embankment. The trooper told me that I must have had an Angel of God with me protecting me. As soon as I was dropped off at home by the State Trooper. I went in the house and went to bed.

Code 224, *the sixth scent*

There was an elite squad of bounty hunters that came to earth to seek revenge for the murders of their people. However, when they arrived on earth they found out that their future rested in their present with all the human beings on earth.

The elite squad of bounty hunters named the sixth scent, were, Milotor, Zuto, Manhattan, Moneybag, Zorax, Keepstack, and Morgannas.

They arrived on earth in a ship sent by the Sphecians of the planet Sphere. Their ship landed on the east river banks of New York City. Undetected they immediately started their hunt that commenced right in Manhattan. They searched for a man by the name of Tony Burton. Tony was a Secret Service Agent that conducted the slaughter of citizens in the planet Sphere. Tony led the attack on that planet that caused the deaths of millions of Sphecians. Therefore, the bounty hunters were on the hunt for the man responsible for these deaths.

At noon right at the banks of the Statute of Liberty, they confronted Tony Burton. As Zuto called Tony, immediately he drew his weapon. The others stood at the banks as Zuto challenged Tony. Tony raised his fist and from the side of this river came other men. Zuto again called Tony to the death by their weapon of choice. As Tony took the challenge his men attacked the other bounty hunters. Outnumbered twenty to six, the bounty hunters fought valiantly.

The bounty hunters clashed violently against their wanted villain. Tony Burton was no ordinary human. He was a member of the clan of Gorgans, a vicious and ruthless race of people that came from the underworld city called Tarmei. They were, kept in check by the earth's galactic government because Tarmei's people were a menace to all living planets in the galaxy.

Agent Burton fought the elite squad of bounty hunters, killing every one of them as the bounty hunters attempted to apprehend the villain. Then out of the shadows of the night, appeared code 224. A galactic force that agent Burton could not defeat. Code 224 struck agent Burton's men with his Sphere blades. He used a galactic Saju sword that cut every man in half. Then there were just the two left. Code 224 versus Tony Burton; and just like that code 224 took agent Burton by the throat, lifted him up in the air and squeezed the life out of his body. It was now over. Next mission!

Code 224-next mission

I drove in my Mercedes Benz CLS 500 into the streets of Waterbury sector red zone. I beeped the horn of my car. He came down from his building. He opened the door of my car while the Techno music was blasting. He had his sunglasses on and he was wearing an Italian leather jacket with matching leather pants and a pair of black boots. I said to him "Let's roll bro." We took off to the city. We got to the Bronx to a place called the rat hole. I parked my car, and popped the trunk open. We got our weapons' a pistol grip shot gun and an M-16 grenade launcher. As we walked through the back alley of the rat hole building, we looked at each other. As we walked through the alley, people recognized us and ran to hide from us. We got to a steel door. Danny grenade launched the door, and made a huge hole on the side of the wall. As we walked in, there were bodies lying on the floor from the blast. We walked to a room and we fought the Dragkens that serve lord Maeska as body guards. Danny and I took care of them as if nothing mattered but to get to their boss. Finally upstairs in their main chamber room, he was there. We walked in. He stared at us with his evil eyes. I struck him with all of my skills, and Danny struck him with his powerful technique. After ten minutes of power fighting. Maeska went down. He went down for the count and could not get up. He was not going to get up. It is the end for him. We thought that he would be one less criminal in this world. We thought that he would never hurt another woman or anyone again. We walked out of the building and got in my car. We drove to the Hutchinson, River, Parkway, then to 684 North then to 84 East directly to Waterbury. I drove up to Danny's neighborhood sector red zone where his home was. He looked at me straight in the eyes. He said later "bro". I replied, "Later". He got out of my car and walked into his building. I drove away. To the next mission!

Code 224-next mission

Blood Friday was a night that the slayers would get together to satisfied their thirst. Tonight, the elite squad of B.E.A. got together for the hunt. T.H.B., Blood hound, Moneybag, Centuria, Stealth, Blaze, and Seeker got in the van. I programmed the car navigation system on hunt mode. We drove to Palace of Desires in Hartford Connecticut. We went to the parking lot. We got out of the van all dressed in black and with our weapons. At around two in the morning, we broke the front door down of this layer of death. As soon as we got in, I started to shoot the bloodsuckers. They fell like flies all over the nightclub's dance floors. Bloodhound became insane as he fought, and killed all the Vampirism creatures that got on his way. He used his rage and animal strength to fight the creatures. With his nine millimeter filled with silver nitrate and holy water bullets, Moneybag shot and killed the blood-sucking creatures on the walls. Centuria was using her martial arts skills to stop anything that moved. While, Stealth and Blaze with their swords killed all the ones flying towards them, and seeker took command of their minds showing us where their leader was. We went to the basement where he was located with his human slaves. I shot their leader with a chemical called Vatiman. Vatiman was a mix of holy water and vampirism dust. Their leader became ill and fell to the ground. We took him out to the van. We tied him up on top of the van. It was five o'clock Saturday morning when we drove off. With the sun out, we stopped the van got out and we looked at the top of the van. All that was left was the ropes and the ashes. To the next mission!

Code 224-next mission

November 14, 2007 and I am chasing a motorcycle. I am on I-84 towards the New York State border. It is just before two in the morning on a Saturday while I am going 180 mph in my Benz. I am enjoying this as I drive faster and faster after this bounty. The bike is streaking her speed as I'm surprising the hell out of the driver. As we approach Pawling New York the driver decides to pull over. I come out of the car and I reach for the back of my trench coat and pull out my 20 gauge pistol grip shot gun (aka Omega Supreme). The driver takes the helmet off and gets off the bike. She stands at around six feet and five inches tall with an athletic built, black hair, deep black eyes and light color skin. I point the weapon at her face and she stares right into my eyes. I request from her to place her hands on her hips as she is trying to hypnotize me. She refuses and tells me her name, Ma-ri-ce-lis. I said to her that I did not ask for her name and I did not care. She again looks at me with her deep black eyes. I say to her that she is under arrest as a bounty is out on her. She laughs, she giggles, and she smiles at me. I show her my hand cuffs that are color black. She takes them and puts them around her wrist and positions herself for a frisk. After frisking her, I take her into my car and I sit her on the front seat where I can keep my eyes on her. As we are driving back to Connecticut, all she does is stare at me. I ask her why she is staring at me so much. Then right when I get off the exit ramp, she tells me to pull over. She took control of the steering wheel and pulls the car over. She opens the door without the hand cuffs that I placed on her. At that point I get out of the car and I go around towards the passenger side of the car. She stands right in front of me and looks at me straight into my eyes. I pull my weapon out of my trench coat. I aim it at her chest. Suddenly, she transforms into a Gorgen. With her wings expanded and ready to fly away. I shot a stun shot at her side. She fell to her knees and then on her back. It is over. I win again, code 224. To the next mission!

Code 224-next mission

The best day of the week is today. Must be like eighty degrees and muggy. Well, in any case I am heading to a place called Bottoms Edge. I called Zorax and Bajeime to meet me at my place. Our mission is to locate and bring back the criminal Stormack McGee, public enemy number one in the city of Salem. I wait for the two blade fighters and off we go into the day and maybe the night. We drive up to the park at exactly three in the afternoon. It is a muggy afternoon and we wonder why the streets are so quiet. We see a group of locals hanging on the corner of West Main Street. We pull over and we ask "where is Stormack?" They respond by telling us that the cruel heartless man is at Bottoms Edge. We go up there and his car is parked in the front of the club. It is six o'clock in the evening and we are staking out the building until dark. Finally, eight thirty in the evening arrives and we get out of the car and approach the night club. The three of us walk into the club and approach a security man. We ask "where is Stormack?" The security man points to the back room. We go to the back room. Stormack sees us as we are facing his body guards. He calls them off as the body guards are surprised by our visit. Stormack turns around and we put the handcuffs on him. We drive off out of the city and head to the holding cage. Mission completed.

Code 224-next mission

It is November 14 2008, Brenda, and I are heading to Club Galaxy 2000. We park in our VIP parking. I get out of the Lexus, and my lady is walking with me towards the front door. Oh yes, she is dressed in a tight Italian black leather pants and jacket that fits like a glove on her. Maximilian, the front entrance bodyguard, says hello to us. He opens the door for us and we go in. Inside the club I see the action that I am looking for. There he is, the man they call 3-D. He stands about six feet seven inches tall weighing around two hundred and twenty pounds, and a shaved head. He is in front of the mirrors standing in a freeze pose when his enemies show up, and start to battle him. He strikes them with all of his skills. In and out I see the shocks of skills that are neutralizing his enemies. I think to myself "he is doing well." "Impressive this young master is in this battle." So I stare and I stare. Then suddenly his enemy's master shows himself. His name is Taze. At this point it is time for me to step in. I now make my move and they all see me approach the floor. He bows in respect with a smile. I signal to him to stand aside. So I say "I am here Taze and it is you and me. Let's bring the old to the new tonight and let us battle." As he brings his skills to the dark floor, I mesmerize him with my eloquent moves. He quickly settles for the first style he has, while I flash move by him. For every move he does I move to a different side of the floor. He looks confused and is breathing heavy. I take off my sunglasses and the glow from my eyes paralyzes this man called Taze. Suddenly, as I approach him I wave to his heart a death blow that sends him twenty feet across the floor. The crowd is stunned and in shock at this move on Taze. I look at him, he is down and done. It is now over for this Taze master.

I look at 3-D; he looks at me, and nods his head in respect with a smile. I grab my girl's hand, and we walk out of the night club. We get into my Lexus and drive off into the night. Battle over. Final mission!

Letters in a Bottle

Centurion Letter

Year Unknown

I am sent by my King to go and find you. I am Teratus, the King's Knight and captain of the guards. He has summoned me to go and find you. It is a quest that has been given to me even if it costs my life. I am in search for you to bring you to my King. He says your beauty is unforgettable. He told me that your eyes are glossy like the blue ocean under the Sun. He told me that your hair is as black silk that could not be compared to any other woman on Earth. My King has instructed me that your sexual presence is real and unique. He told me that your skin is fair and golden like the brass in the halls of our Kingdom. I have been told that I am to bring you back to my King's presence. I have been told that your beauty is like no other woman's beauty. My King has told me to bring you back to his chamber where he sits waiting for you. Did you know that our city is built around your beauty? I have been told to search for you. Not just for him but for our city, our country and our people. I was told that everyone loves you and that you are the best and that you are different. I was told that you are gentle, and that your heart is good and full of grace. I was told that you are talented and forever unforgettable. I have never met you but I will see that this request gets accomplished. I am the King's best. I have never failed my King. My lady, I will find you. It is my life's duty to accomplish my quest. I am on my way around the world to find you, my lady, my beautiful Boricua queen. Rest and wait where you are. The King has sent me to find you and I am going to be there soon. Centurion Teratus Maxus

February 2, 2012

Maduxx Battalion
Freedom Fighter
Michael Storm 224

Dear Sheila,
My squad and I were sent on a mission to destroy a machine factory. To tell you the truth that was my first mission. I have only been in this war for two days and I already feel home sick. Nevertheless, we went into a city called Bridgeport that is in Connecticut. We are not too far from the New York sector. Not that it really matters because the destruction is the same everywhere. We approached the assembly factory from its north side on a Sunday morning at around five. As we approached the plant, we came across machines that walked and acted like human soldiers. They were fully equipped with heavy gun fire and looked as evil as anything you could imagine from hell. We scrambled aggressively with heavy gunfire on each of the factory's main buildings and its outlets. We destroyed hundreds of machines and we were able to destroy the whole factory. During the course of our attack, we suffered some casualties. Gary Johnson was a soldier that was at my right hand side when he was gunned down by a machine. One second he was next to me giving me a signal to attack and the next his body exploded when it got hit by a Centurion gun laser fire. There is so much destruction all over that I wonder at times if we are really fighting for anything of value. There are rumors that we are loosing the war all over the world. It takes years to produce and to build a human soldier while it takes the machines a few hours to assemble a fully armed unit. I am not to sure my love if I will make it out of this hell hole.

I already miss you very much and I am writing to you as I promised I would. I hope you are ok and that you are laying low. I have you in my heart my love. Always remember that I am thinking of you.

Faithfully,
Mike Storm 224

August 1, 2012

Maduxx Battalion
Storm 224

Dear Sheila,

This week I was assigned to the Vermont sector of the North East region. There is a lot of snow up in the mountains of Vermont. Being that I am from the Florida sector, I am not used to the cold and the freezing temperatures that exist here. The status for us is as usual stable and in operation. Our Sergeant, Theresa Guzman is new with us and she is as tough as they come. Although the men talk a lot of crap about her, I am glad that she is with us. I feel safe with her style of combat. She doesn't trust anyone and the scars on her face, tells me of her experience on the battle field. We are driving plasma tanks to confront and destroy the Glaston blast ships that the machines have in this area. So far we have not encountered any hostiles. I think it is just the weather that is not allowing the machines to maneuver freely. I really don't care because I just want to get this war over with and go home. The other night we were raided by underground machines and fifteen of our freedom marine soldiers were killed. The machines were shaped like wild dogs and cats. Since it was night time, we were able to see their red eyes. We scrambled to the mountains for cover and managed to escape these machines. When the raid was over, and the smoke cleared it was not a pretty site. There was so much death and destruction that I was sick to my stomach. At sun up as we came down from the mountains, there were dead bodies and body parts everywhere. I just could not stomach the smell of death all over the battlefield. Sheila, how are you my love? I wish I could see you. Even if it is for ten minutes, that would be a life times worth. I hope that you and the kids are ok and that your sector is holding on strong. Maybe this war will be over soon whether in victory or defeat. The burden of this War feels so heavy at times that I just want for it to end. In any case Sheila, God speed.

Truly,
Mike Storm 224

December 24, 2013

Maduxx Battalion
Freedom Fighter
Storm 224

Dear Sheila,

I cannot help but to spend this evening thinking of you and our town. I know it is been over a year since I last wrote to you. However, as you already know we were sent to a highly classified mission under the Atlantic Ocean and no communication with the rest of the country was allowed. All this was because of the new F-1000 spy machines that came out at the same time that I last wrote to you. The machines were intercepting all communications from humans around the country. So we were ordered to pipe down on writing letters and radio talk. I am glad that order was called off last week. I am here looking at your picture. We have been given the night to stay low and rest. Although our commanders are being considerate because it is Christmas Eve, it is very sad for us. My Sheila, I hope that you are doing well. I hope that you have not forgotten of the love that we have for each other. I miss you very much. I miss our talks, our walks and our moments of love. I remember looking into your beautiful eyes and getting completely lost in them. I remember touching your beautiful face and admiring your beauty. Sheila, I remember as I kissed you over and over again how we would hug each other. I remember your beautiful hair how it looked when it was wet. I have to smile because you look like a queen to me. Sheila, I feel so lost while participating in this War. So much has been lost since the War started. All my friends like Carlos, Rey, Tommy, and Rick have been killed on duty. Remember

Jennifer from our neighborhood? She was assigned to my platoon and on a Saturday morning she was killed by a machine patrol ship. At this point, I do not even know if my brothers Hector and Sotero are alive. Last, I knew they were off the coast of Cuba in command of Freedom Navy assault ships. As far as my nephews, the last I heard Eric, Chris, and Trooper where up in the Canada region assigned to a special cobra unit conducting assassination missions. It was two years ago to this day that I last heard from them. I miss my family a lot. Sheila, please let me know at how you are doing. I have heard that the Florida area was hit hard by the machines. That has got me worried for you my love. I miss you greatly. You should know that I was given a promotion in ranking to Sergeant of six stripes. I guess that promotion does not matter if I do not make it home alive. My love, if I do not make it through this War. Remember that I love you deeply and forever. Even though we are far away from each other, my heart is close to you. I miss you as this Christmas evening is coming to an end. Don't forget about me. Don't forget that I love you.

Truly yours,
Mike Storm 224

July 17, 2016

Commander Storm 007
Maduxx Special Unit
Sector East coast USA
Freedom Fighter

Dear Sheila,
I write this letter to you to let you know what has happened so far. We have taken over the sector prime of the machines. Our combat units have performed well and have taken over vital territories in this war. We have delivered a blow to the enemy as we have found their main brain computer and destroyed it. The soldier machines that are operational still, are no longer a threat to us. Because of this great victory freedom fighters from all over have come out to the sun light. We have not been out in the Sun for so many years because of the machines. Furthermore, the rays of the sun are deadly from the nuclear fallout, so we have to be careful. We remember all of those men, women and children that have given their lives to bring back humanity to where it should be. I know that you are there waiting for me and for us. So I am writing to you to let you know that we are on our way. I am so sorry that it is been a few years since my last letter to you. As you might already know, we got ordered to close out all communications with our loved ones. Stay in good cheers and know that we have almost won this war. The machines are devastated at this time without their great brain computer. This is a blow to their capabilities to manufacture more mechanical soldiers. I cannot wait to see you all. The last time I saw you it was four years ago. A lot has happened since then and I know that you have been occupied contributing your part to this war against the machines. I still have your picture and carry it with me every day. I have a few

more scars than what I had when we last saw each other, so don't be alarmed when you see me again. Sheila, remember the days when we were in school? Remember the days when we used to go to the beach, and ride on my motorcycle, and we had all the fun that two people could ever have? Remember that? Most likely we will never experience those days again because of this war. However, rest assured that someday, future generations of humanity will have the opportunity to have that on earth again. It feels good to have been a part of this victory. We are going to perform our last efforts in destroying what is left of the machines. I will be heading home soon once my orders are fulfilled. I write to you because I am anxious to see you my love. I have almost forgotten to what it is to be with a woman and a woman like you. I remember all the nights we spent with each other. I remember the conversations out by the beach, as we were hugged by the ocean breeze. I remember the times when we went to the lovers' site in our town and we would talk all night long until we would fall asleep. I remember looking into your eyes, and getting completely lost in them. I remember kissing your lips and feeling that tingling sensation all over. I remember holding you close to my chest and admiring your presence. I remember the moments of love that we had all those years. I remember the nights when we made love, and I would sketch your body in my heart so that it would never erase itself. I cannot tell you my love at how much I remember and at how much I miss you. This war has almost consumed my life and it has taken so much from all of us. I will be home soon, that I can tell you. I will turn in my ranking position to my commanders in the very near future. I will be home soon, very soon. Until then my love, take care as this journey is coming to an end and a new one is to begin.

Truly yours,
Freedom fighter,
Mike Storm 224

July 25, 2016

Freedom Fighter
Maduxx Command
Michael Storm 224

Dear Donald and Maria Scheiler,
I write this letter to inform you that your son has lost his life while performing his duty defending this world. Corporal J.R. Scheiler was a man with great courage, and while performing his duty as a soldier for this world of ours, he managed to save many freedom fighter marines. His life was lost on the battlefield code name Normandy and the marines in unit Storm 224 served as witnesses of the bravery that he demonstrated. Nothing can replace the loss of a son, a father, a brother or of a friend. We recognize the loss of your son and stand by your side at this time of mourning and grief. Our heavenly father is a witness that our soldiers have stood in truth to their duty to deliver the world from tyranny and oppression. We greatly recognize and appreciate your son's sacrifice to this world. Mr. and Mrs. Scheiler, I the Secretary of defense George C. Marshall III place this great moment in our Lord's hands. Please, know that your son is a hero to our world and will forever be remembered as such. His commanding officer Lieutenant Michael Storm has reported to me and to his other superior officers, that your son was given the Purple Heart burial ceremony. That service was conducted in secrecy and in silence as our cover from our enemy could not be disclosed. Your son will also be awarded the Medal of Honor. His name will be written on the Walls of Remembrance along with all the other brave men and women that have given their lives for freedom.
Sincerely yours,
Secretary of Defense
George C. Marshall III
Freedom Fighters

December 12, 2021

Maduxx Special Unit
Sector East coast USA
Freedom Fighter Storm 224

Dear Sheila Comorey,
The beginning was very difficult. I cannot remember the last time that I saw all of you. It is a long journey back home. I find myself at times on the run for nothing. Although, I am here on this island of death and hell, I can tell you that I hunger for love. I know that I have a duty to perform and that is the reason why I am here on this death island. Nevertheless, say hello to the kids for me. Let them know that their uncle loves them and that I will be home someday after the War is completely over. Although we have defeated the machines, cleaning the last stronghold of the enemy has been difficult. The machines are scattered all over in pockets of what they have now become a resistance. However, they are as any fighting force not going down without a fight. Their inability to produce soldier machines has created a certain defeat for them. Soon we will outlast them, and hunt them down completely until there are no more machine soldiers left. As far as Hollywood (Carlos), I can only tell you that he was a good soldier. He conducted his duty with honor and integrity. On the battle field he fought valiantly. He gave his life to save those that were wounded. Under heavy Centurion fire, Hollywood managed to get as many of our Marine Freedom Fighters out of danger. Tell his friends, and his family that his body will be taken back home soon. The truth is that transportation is provided only by foot as the enemy has destroyed all the available transporting vehicles. I cannot tell you at how much I desire to eat Mom's

cooking and play some dominoes. That is if Mom is ok. I am only allowed to write to other warrior Marines and no one else. If you come across my mom tell her I love her. I wonder at times how many mothers are no longer around. It is been nine years and I am about done with this War. If they would release me, I would go home now. In any case, give my love to everyone in the family. See you soon and remember if you are coming here to this hell hole? You better be ready to suffer like I have.

Cordially yours,
Michael Storm 224

March 29, 2022

Combat unit 224
Maduxx Battalion
Sector East Coast USA

Dear Sheila,

I hope that when you receive this letter you find yourself in good places. Shortly after the War had ended we found out that our commander and chief the great John C. Maduxx had been assassinated by one of the soldier machines. Commander Maduxx conducted a final assault on the machines that pretty much ended their stronghold in this world. Shortly after, he was killed by a machine that he programmed to assist him and the army to win the war. It is a sad day for all of us here as we have received this kind of news. However, it is official; the War has come to a complete end. Even though we have won the War we reflect on the cost and the loss of lives that we have suffered to accomplish such a victory. Commander Maduxx's sacrifice in this war reminds us of what it took to allow humanity to survive. I am so happy to know that I am now truly on my way home to Florida. I have received word from one of the southern commanding centers that Florida is coming out of the nuclear fall out and that the Sun's rays have been peaking through the gray clouds for the past year. Sheila, you should know that I am a different man. This war has changed me to the point where I have been humbled to appreciate life and this world. I cannot tell you at how much I want to be by your side. I want to hold you, and kiss you. I received your letter three weeks ago and I have read it more than one hundred times. I cannot help but to read your letters over and over as it eases my desperation to get to you. Your letters are poetry to me. I feel your heart beat in every word that you have written. I am happy that you are still in the Miami area. I have heard at how the Southern States like Florida's freedom fighters have totally given hell to the machines. I am pleased to hear of the victories that the Southern States have had on the machines even though the Nuclear fall out has been brutal there. My dear Sheila, Know that I am on my way, even as you are reading this letter. I should be arriving in the next month or so. I am so desperate to be there. I am in need of a new life. I feel that although I am alive that I am dead in this world. At times I feel as if there is no hope for mankind. I cannot even remember at how to pray to God anymore. I still have the bible that you gave to me for my twenty fifth birthday and I have read it more than a thousand times. God, it is really hard to believe that I am now thirty four years old. I feel so old and worn out. All I have seen for years is death and destruction. Now that the war is over, I hope that things will be different. However, the restructuring of this world is going to be a challenge of its own. Nevertheless, I am willing to move forward with the next phase of this task. The new Government has encouraged us and has provided every male and female with the necessary education to reproduce. That is the first order given to us so that we can exist in this world. I wonder at times if that is wise with all the nuclear fall out and diseases on this earth. Sheila, hold strong my love because I am coming home. I will be there soon. Do not write back to me because I am on my way to you. If you write to me I will not receive the letter since I am in route to you. I cannot wait to see you.

Truly yours,
Michael Storm 224

June 9, 2022

Combat unit 224
Maduxx Battalion

Dear Sheila,

I hope and pray that as you receive this letter that you and the kids are ok. I want you to know that I was side tracked while heading to Florida. As you already know my journey or rather our journey as there were eight of us heading home, has been interrupted by us being ambushed by stragglers. I caught a bullet wound to my middle section. I am being treated at a hospital barracks in the Baltimore, MA region. I woke up one morning there and the doctor told me that it would be a month before I can walk or hike long distance. I sent this letter with a high ranking personnel freight carrier heading your way. It all started when we managed to catch a transport from the New York City area to Philadelphia. From that point we started on foot to Florida. It was going well until we reached the Baltimore region and got ambushed. I think I will be ok. It is just that I am desperate to be home and be with you. The others that traveled with me were Joe, Michael, Steve, Dan, Meggen, Jason, Elias and Kelly. They were also freedom fighter marines and that had decided to travel with us. I received the sad news that Michael and Dan were killed in the ambush. The others were wounded but survived and are somewhere in the city of Baltimore. I don't know if I will be traveling together with them any time soon. I do know however, that soon I will be heading to Florida. Sheila my love, soon we will be together again. I am almost there sweetheart. I can almost see the moment where we will be together again. Until then my love, be strong and know that I am on my way. Give a hug and a kiss to the kids for me and tell them that uncle Mike is on his way home. I love you always.

Truly yours
Mike Storm 224

July 2, 2022

Unit 0073
Comorey Rough Necks
Freedom Fighter
Southern Eastern Sector

Dear Michael,

I am writing to you because I have received word that you have been killed and that you were taken to Newport News, Virginia. I do not really understand why you are taking so long to get home. Now that the War is over and my duties as a commanding officer are less demanding. I have requested to pursue after you my love with my squadron, the Rough Necks. We left just after June 1, out of Florida. I decided to write this letter to you and send it with a freight carrier escorted by the legendary Deadly Vipers and Eagles Rage unit that was heading to the Washington area. Meeting them was a great experience because I or rather we had never met those warriors that have been legendary throughout this War. It was amazing to see their armor, their warrior look and their demeanor as they spoke to us. We could not travel with them because they were on a highly classified mission. Nevertheless, I asked their Lieutenant, Jason Tree Cormier to deliver this letter for me. The lieutenant told me that he would do that for me as he was headed through the Virginia area. I had never met a freedom fighter that was seven feet tall like Lt. Cormier. As long as he delivers the letter, that is all that matters to me. My love if you receive this letter before I get to you, please make sure that you stay alive. I don't believe in my heart that you have been killed. My heart tells me different and I am pursuing that heart felt feeling. I have received all of your letters and

I have lived all of these days, months and years with them in my vest pocket. Michael, don't do anything stupid to hurt yourself more than what you are injured. I spoke to a Marine private Kelly out of Tampa and she told me that she was in the ambush that you and that group suffered. She told me at how you fought against the stragglers. She explained to me at how you single handily killed seven of the stragglers in the hopes to defend your group. Kelly also told me at how you stood in front of a gun shot to save her and two others. Michael you never change my love. The war has not changed you Michael Storm. All it did was make you stronger and more powerful. I also received a report from a general Bradley Gamera that you were highly decorated for your success in all the missions that you and your squadron were assigned to. It does not surprise me at your bravery and your talent as a Freedom Fighter Marine. I'm on my way my love. Hold strong Marine, because I have waited for you all these years and I want you back with me.

Faithfull yours,
Sheila Comorey

July 22, 2022

Storm 224
Freedom Fighter Marine

Dear Sheila,
I regret to inform you that I am not able to get home at this time. I have
Been severely injured and cannot walk. My body is broken and I am as you already know pretty much dead. The doctors have informed me that they cannot repair me and that I don't have much time to live. I am bleeding internally and I cannot breathe any more. I have asked a nurse to write this letter for me as I am not able to write. My fingers are not functioning at all and my legs are paralyzed. I was reported as dead. I am here Sheila at a town called Hampton in Virginia. I was in a shuttle freight carrier heading to Florida when it lost an engine and went down in the Virginia area. The crash broke my back, legs and left me paralyzed. I am also bleeding internally and the doctors cannot stop it. So I am on life support for the meantime. Oh Sheila, I am so sorry that I have failed you my love. I never made it to you. I love you Sheila. If you get this letter please know that my heart was always yours. I held you day and night in my arms. I love you Sheila and I am thankful for the times we had together. I cannot any longer take the pain in my body and in my heart. I wish I could see you one last time. I wish I could hold you one last time. I wish I could kiss your lips one last time. I am done here on this earth. Now, I surrender myself to my destiny. Sheila, live long on this earth and help it move forward to full restoration. Tell everyone that I love them very much. I am forever yours.

Truly,
Michael Storm 224

Street Soldier

Year Unknown
Bronx New York
Re: Latin night at the *Latin Palace*

Dear Brenda,
I want to let you know that I miss talking to you. Your presence is inviting and pleasant to me. Your beauty is exotic and tempting. Your love is curious and deadly. For that I live on the edge of life wanting the excitement of ones fantasy and life's ventures. So I ask princess of beauty, can you take my heart? I am a street soldier and I am headed your way. I wonder how your state of physicality is. You are an amazing woman. In some Universe, you have been known to be a Goddess, and in some worlds' you have been called a Queen. In many other places, you have been called a Sapphire of beauty. To me I pronounce you and your beauty in my heart. I am a street soldier and I am headed your way.

Yours truly,
S.S.

Letter

Sis, here are some documents about Papi that I got as I am writing a book about him titled The American Dancer. I have as I am trying to complete this project, come to the conclusion that we are all forever hurt on earth on the loss of our father. His death has impacted this family in such a way, that I am certain that Mayda and Carlos went on to be with the Lord because of his absence. Although, we can die of a disease or an accident, the heart does not lie. I remember one day just before Carlos passing away, at how he wrote poems about Papi. His poems expressed to me how much he missed him. With Mayda, in her last few months of life, she would tell me stories about him and would start to cry. She would tell me that if she was to die she would be with Papi. Once she even said to me "it would not be that bad." All this time I never really understood why they would say such things. However, now as I am attempting to write this book and as I read these documents, I see Papi's resume of his life. To be able to read his decorations in the Army with medals and his parents names on these documents, gives me a sense of peace. I cannot lie to you both, every night I try to write about him and the tears come out. There are times that I wish that he would be here with us still so that I could have a chance at being a better son to him. I wish I had appreciated him better than what I did, when he was alive. He did so much in his time as a man in this world. He always tried to do what was right with the little that he had and the little that he knew. He was an orphan, a fighter, a warrior in the Army, a survivor and most of all he was a good father. I don't think that we could actually accept the fact that he is not here any longer. It hurts even to this day which is almost ten years later. The other day when I was being taken into the operating room, I thought to myself that if I would die, it would not be so bad because I would be with Papi. At that moment I found myself making the same statements to myself as Mayda and Carlos did. I also understand why I go to Puerto Rico so much. Junior kind of answered the question the other night, when he said "seen Uncle Victor is not easy." I think that what happened was that when Junior saw Uncle Victor, he reminded him of Papi. I remember that night when we were at the resort and Junior saw Uncle Victor I saw tears in his eyes. I could not help it but when I got back to our suite I went into my room and broke down. I thought to myself at how much I missed Papi. So, when I got these documents I understood that I go to Puerto Rico because Uncle Victor looks like him so much that I feel good being there with him. Life is hard, especially when the ones you love so much are gone. I guess that we have to look no further in our lives we can be content and hold true that God has given us everything we will ever need. That is our family. It all started with Mami and Papi. Hold these documents and read them. As you read them you will able to see grandma and grandpa whom we never met. From that point on everything else will make sense.

Yours Truly,
Your Brother

Wall of Writers

A Writer of Time
Decoy
Trooper
Danny Dan
Lyrics of Ink
Scientific
3-D
Tutor Man
Scripto
Last Poet
The Last Writer
V.R.V Victor Rivera Vazquez
Twilight Writer
Passionate
Street law
Megens Fury
Megens Love
Romantic
Lady Aline
Smurf Writer

About the Author

Born in NY/ NY

Of Puerto Rican parents

Graduated from Western Connecticut State University

Half Raised in Bronx NY and in Danbury Connecticut

Edwin enjoys writing poetry, short stories, science fiction, playing sports, and enjoys listening to music.

Is an entrepreneur.

Edwin has written music for Rainbow Records.

Titles: Happy Holidays songs *Christmas Night, Forever Christmas.*

Also with Rainbow Records title: Hollywood Gold, songs *I Love You, The First Time.*

Other writing projects, National Library of Poetry, poem *Decision.*

Book author *A Writer of Time* published 2007

Favorite place to vacation: Puerto Rico (Cabo Rojo, Boquerón)

Favorite Book: The Holy Bible

Favorite Movie: Chisum (John Wayne)

Favorite Music: Christian Worship Songs and Salsa

Favorite singer: *Sade (your music moves my soul to write)*

Would you like to see your manuscript become a book?

If you are interested in becoming a PublishAmerica author, please submit your manuscript for possible publication to us at:

acquisitions@publishamerica.com

You may also mail in your manuscript to:

**PublishAmerica
PO Box 151
Frederick, MD 21705**

www.publishamerica.com

CPSIA information can be obtained at www.ICGtesting.com
Printed in the USA
BVOW09s2247110214

344652BV00001B/69/P

9 781456 064556